Cherry Home

Companion

I Spend My Summers In
CHERRYLAND
Why Don't You?

GRAND TRAVERSE REGION, MICHIGAN

Cherry Home Companion

Patty LaNoue Stearns

Book design: Susan Bays

Library of Congress Cataloging in Publication Data available

ISBN 0-9665316-5-5

Arbutus Press
P.O. Box 234
Mayfield, Michigan 49686

www.Arbutuspress.com

10 9 8 7 6 5 4 3 2 1

First Edition
Printed in Korea

Cover: Orson W. Peck produced thousands of postcards of Northern Michigan from 1890 until his death in 1954. He altered most of his photos to produce composites. Peck hand-colored many of his early postcards. Prior to 1914, they were produced from a large view-camera using glass-plate negatives.

To my sisters, Judy, Nancy and Linda,
Who shared the branches of our cherry tree

And to my mom, Irene Evelyn Mitscha LaNoue,
who made sure our lives would never be the pits

———

SINCERE THANKS TO OUR RECIPE TESTERS

The OB Nursing Staff at Martin Memorial Hospital, Stuart, FL, made this book a cross-country cherry jubilee: Susan Brown, Lisa Christopher, Angela Dowd, Elsa Jerdeman, Paula Kelly, Dee Krueger and her daughter Kim Beckett, Marilyn Martin, Heidi Nichols, Michelle Parolski, and Nancy Wagoner (my sister).

Jackie Cobb and Jacquie Honea of Jacquie Caters, Traverse City.

And to our postcard scouts and general cheerleaders: Susan Wilcox Olson, Director of Marketing, National Cherry Festival; Village Press, Traverse City; Kathi Waggoner Gober, Midland; Doris Waggoner, Acme; Fred Laughlin, Director of the Culinary School at Northwestern Michigan College, Traverse City; Gail Lange, owner of The Cherry Stop, Traverse City; Ted Bays and Joe Stearns, caregivers, and to the chefs and food writers who contributed such fabulous recipes.

CHERRIES

Contents

Sweet (And Sticky) Memories

Cherries have always been a sweet part of my life, starting with the fruits of the fertile tree in our big backyard in the Detroit suburb of Allen Park, Michigan. The tree grew near the fence, next to an alley, and when spring arrived we would measure the days before summer by the vibrant green buds that filled the branches.

As those buds blossomed into a much-too-fleeting show of fragrant pale-pink flowers, we knew that vacation time — and baskets and baskets of juicy fruit — were not far behind. The tree bore rich, ripe, shiny orbs in early summer and was the perfect size for climbing. My sisters and I sat among the branches that overlooked our yard, giggling and plucking the deep-red spheres from their stems one by one, eating as many as we could swallow, spitting the pits, sticky juice running down our chins, our necks, the fronts of our blouses. Sometimes we'd fall from the branches, adding blood to our already discolored hands and clothing, but it was summer, after all, and my mother forgave us.

Besides, she wanted to stay on our good side. Mom needed our help with harvesting, pitting and canning. We had other fruit trees in our yard — peaches, apples and plums — but cherries were our favorite. My grandmother would come with her amazing stainless-steel machine that would poke out the pits and extrude the cherries almost whole. We'd put up millions of them, it seemed, in big quart jars, and eat them the rest of the year in pies, tarts and jelly, but mostly just by themselves.

When I got a little older, around 12, I picked tart cherries for pin money while vacationing at my family's cottage near the Silver Lake Sand Dunes in western Michigan's Oceana County. I didn't make a whole lot — 50 cents a 25-pound lug, which took me a couple of hours to amass under a hot July sun — but it gave me a hands-on appreciation for the value of cherries and how they get to our tables.

As a summer ritual, we'd stop at the cherry stand in Shelby on the road to our Lake Michigan cottage for the fragrant cherry pies, turnovers and strudel that Barb Bull's family made. The proceeds from all those products sold at Cherry Point Farm Market put Barb's sister Marilyn through medical school. She's now at the University of Indiana, specializing in developmental pediatrics, and Barb still runs the family farm and the stand — which has turned into a burgeoning restaurant, the Cherry Point Garden Grill, with a winery, organic produce and herb garden, and soon, a Bed and Breakfast Inn.

In my long career as a journalist, I've written about Barb Bull and others who live their lives doing the cherry dream. And now I, too, am living it in Traverse City, Cherry Capital of the World. Cherries are almost daily staples in my repertoire — on cereal, salads, main courses, side dishes and of course, desserts.

In putting together this book it was our intention to assemble the most delicious cherry recipes we could find — anywhere. I believe we have done it. We scoured cookbooks, magazines, recipe databases, and best of all asked countless chefs and culinary experts for their most innovative cherry creations. The result is more than 150 mouthwatering ways to eat the fruit that launched a billion pies — and still counting.

Here's to all your cherry dreams.

Cherry Chat

- Michigan is the nation's leading producer of tart cherries—70 to 75 percent of the crop each year, or 200 to 250 million pounds. Utah is next with 8 percent of the crop; New York, about 5 percent; Wisconsin, 4 percent. Washington, Oregon and Pennsylvania also have commercial crops of tart cherries.

- Montmorency is the major tart cherry variety grown in the United States.

- Tart cherries are seldom sold fresh; they generally are canned, frozen or dried shortly after harvesting.

- There are about 7,000 tart cherries on an average tree; that's enough cherries for about 28 pies.

- The average U.S. citizen consumes about one pound of tart cherries per year. That is more than 260 million pounds per year.

- Sweet cherries primarily are grown in the Pacific Coast states. Michigan joins the top four producers, harvesting about 20 percent — or 50 million pounds — of the crop each year.

- The most famous sweet cherry variety is the Bing cherry. However, there are more than 1,000 varieties of sweet cherries. Bing cherries are a dark red / burgundy color. There also are light sweet cherry varieties, such as Rainier and Queen Anne.

- Both tart and sweet cherries ripen in July; the third week of July is usually the peak of the harvest.

Source: Cherry Marketing Institute

Cherry Handling

- **Storing**

  Select firm, red, tree-ripened fruits. Store unwashed ripe cherries in refrigerator uncovered and use within three to five days.

- **Canning**

  Rinse, drain and remove stems and pits, if desired. Pack cherries into clean hot canning jars and cover with medium-hot syrup ($1^1/2$ cups sugar to 2 cups water), leaving $1/2$-inch headspace. Seal according to manufacturer's directions. Place jars on rack in canner. Process 25 minutes for pints and quarts in boiling water bath with boiling water two inches above jar tops. Remove jars from canner. Cool away from drafts. Remove rings from sealed jars after 12 hours. At high altitudes processing times vary. For more information, see USDA Information Bulletin #539 or call your local county cooperative extension office.

- **Freezing**

  Stem, sort and wash thoroughly. Drain and pit. The syrup-pack method is best for cherries that will be served uncooked; sugar pack is preferable for pies or other cooked products.

- **Syrup pack**

  Pack cherries into containers and cover with cold 50-percent syrup, (1 cup water to 1 cup sugar), depending on the tartness of the cherries. Seal, label and freeze.

- **Sugar pack**

  To 1 quart ($1^1/3$ pounds) cherries add $3/4$ cup sugar. Mix until sugar is dissolved. Pack into containers. Seal, label and freeze.

- **Drying**

  Wash and cut fruits in half and remove pits. Dry 24 to 36 hours in a dehydrator. Properly dried cherries are leathery and shriveled.

Sources: Michigan State University Extension and Washington State Fruit Commission

Cherry Etiquette

The pit of the fruit should be made as clean as possible in your mouth and then dropped into your almost closed, cupped hand and thence to your plate. When you remove a pit with your fingers, you should do it with your thumb underneath and your first two fingers across your mouth, and not with your fingertips pointing into your mouth. If you prefer, pits can be pushed forward with the tongue onto a spoon and then dropped onto a plate.

Emily Post's *Etiquette, 16th Edition*, Harper Collins Publishers, 1997

Cherry Festivals

The Nago City Cherry Blossom Festival, January, Okinawa, Japan
Sakura Matsuri (cherry-blossom festival), March and April, Tokyo, Japan
Macon, Georgia International Cherry Blossom Festival, mid-March
National Cherry Blossom Festival, late March-early April, Washington, DC
Seattle Cherry Blossom & Japanese Cultural Festival, mid-April, Seattle, Washington
Vignola Cherry Festival, mid May-early June, Emilia Romana, Italy
Tekirdag Cherry Festival, early June, Tekirdag, Turkey
Cherry Valley Festival, June, Cherry Valley, California
Washington's Fruit Place Cherry Festival, late June, Yakima, Washington
Festival of Cherries, July, Fougerolles, Haute-Saonne, France
Eau Claire Cherry Festival, July 4, Eau Claire, Wisconsin
National Cherry Festival, early July, Traverse City, Michigan
Bear River Cherry Carnival, mid-to late July, Bear River, Nova Scotia, Canada
Westhoffen Cherry Festival, in Alsance west of Strasbourg, third weedend of July
National Cherry Festival, early December, New South Wales, Australia

Cherry Measure

One pound of fresh cherries is equal to 3 cups stemmed and $2\,1/2$ cups pitted. One pound of frozen cherries equals about 3 cups; 4 to 5 cups of tart cherries make one pie. There are about $2^1/3$ cups cherry pie filling in a 21-ounce can and about 2 cups of tart cherries in a 16-ounce can. One pound of dried tart cherries equals about $3\,1/2$ cups.

Cherry Pits

No pitter? No problem. Try a drinking straw to push the pit out the stem end, a clean needle-nose pliers, the tip of a vegetable peeler or a sharp knife, or even the end of a paper clip.

Cherry Quickies

Bread stuffing, pilaf, pudding, and oatmeal: Add $1/4$ cup dried tart cherries to your favorite recipe for more zip.

Candy treat: Melt semisweet chocolate or white chocolate chips over low heat. Stir in dried cherries. Add toasted almonds, if desired. Mix until coated with chocolate. Spoon onto waxed paper.

Pie panache: Add 1 cup of dried cherries to traditional cherry pie to increase the cherry flavor. Or add about $1/2$ cup dried tart cherries to your favorite apple or peach pie recipe. The cherries complement the other fruit while adding flavor and color.

Trail mix: Try a combination of dried cherries, banana chips, chocolate chips and peanuts.

Snack food: Tuck packages of dried tart cherries into lunch boxes.

Cherries: A Short History

Imagine the discovery of a fine spreading tree with small, shiny, seductive red fruits.

One can only guess at the excitement, or perhaps trepidation, of that first bite. Was it sour or sweet, ripe or still firm? Did an adventuresome eater round up a group and do an official tasting, or was it a solo act of blind gustatory passion?

We will never know. Some date that discovery at 300 BC in what is now the province of Giresun on the Black Sea coastline of Turkey. Giresun was called Cerasus, the source of the scientific name for sour cherries. Cherries are a subgenus within *Prunus*, shared with plums, apricots, peaches and almonds — all part of the Rosaceae family. Sweet cherries are *Prunus avium* and sour, *Prunus cerasus*.

Long a symbol of chastity and virginity (the round red fruit with enclosed seed symbolizing the uterus), the cherry has other fascinating folklore attached to it. An old wives' tale in Europe, for example, says that the owner of a cherry tree could be sure of having a rich crop of fruit if the first cherry to ripen was eaten by a woman who recently gave birth to her first child.

Danish folklore held that forest demons lived in cherry trees. Serbian mystical fairies supposedly sang and danced among the cherry trees.

It is known that the Greeks and Romans cultivated sour cherries some 2,000 years ago. Other evidence suggests Etruscans may have grown sweet cherries. In more recent history, early American settlers brought them here by ship in the 1600s, and sour cherries grew in Thomas Jefferson's first orchard at Monticello.

Cherry pits were planted along the Saint Lawrence River and on down into the Great

Lakes area by French colonists from Normandy, who used them to ornament their gardens in Detroit and other settlements in the Midwest.

Early Grand Traverse region pioneers planted cherry trees on their homesteads and found the trees producing an abundance of fruit. The area proved ideal for growing cherries because Lake Michigan tempers winter's Arctic winds and cools the orchards in summer. The trees flourished, and soon other area farmers became cherry cheerleaders, too.

Michigan's first commercial tart cherry orchards were planted in 1893 on Ridgewood Farm. Ten years later, the tart cherry industry had spread along Lake Michigan's coastline, all the way from Elk Rapids to Benton Harbor.

The Montmorency, the primary tart cherry variety, was planted in the early orchards and is still used today.

Cherries also sweetened the Pacific Northwest. In 1847, Henderson Lewelling planted an orchard in western Oregon, using nursery stock that he transported by ox cart from Iowa. His most famous sweet cherry variety is the Bing, named by one of Lewelling's Chinese workmen. Another sweet cherry, Lambert, also got its start on Lewelling Farms. Bing, Lambert and Rainier, developed in Washington State, account for more than 95 percent of Northwest sweet cherries.

Maraschinos, the bright-red blobs used in drinks and on ice cream sundaes, are made from sweet cherries. The maraschino originated in Yugoslavia and northern Italy, where merchants added a liqueur to a local cherry called the Marasca. But it was Americanized and de-alcoholized, and by 1920 its color and almond flavor were nothing like the original. The most recent innovation is the dried tart cherry, which makes eating cherries a delicious year-round affair and Balaton is the newest American tart cherry variety. Developed by Dr. Amy Iezzoni at Michigan State University, the Balaton has great potential for the fresh market and for juice.

Health benefits of cherries are another recent discovery. At least 17 compounds in tart cherries have antioxidant properties. Antioxidants can help slow down, prevent or repair damage done to the body's cells by free radicals. According to ongoing research, cherries can help fight cancer and heart disease. In addition, there are beneficial compounds in Montmorency tart cherries that help relieve the pain of arthritis and gout. While the research is ongoing, consumers are using tart cherry juice and other cherry products to stave off pain.

Around the world, the cherry is celebrated for its beautiful flowers, ornamental foliage, vibrant fruit and the signal that summer has arrived. In Michigan, the National Cherry Festival in July fills the streets and waterfront parkways of the Cherry Capital of the World, Traverse City, Michigan. From a spring ceremony known as the "Blessing of the Blossoms" first held in 1925, it has blossomed into a world-class celebration with a huge parade, fabulous floats and thousands of cherry fans every year.

Sources: Cherry Marketing Institute, Inc., Mystical World Wide Web

Cherry Types: Sweet

- Bing: Large, firm, juicy, sweet, nearly black when ripe — superb flavor, the No.1 cherry.

- Black Tartarian: Medium-sized, nearly black, sprightly flavor, early season.

- Craig's Crimson: Perhaps the finest sweet cherry; dark red to nearly black, medium to large size, wonderful spicy flavor, very firm texture.

- Lambert: Large, black, late harvest. Highest quality, rivaling Bing.

- Lapins: New, from Canada. Dark red sweet cherry. Large, firm, good flavor.

- Rainier: Large, yellow with red blush. Sweet and flavorful, superior to Royal Ann.

- Royal Ann: Long-time favorite yellow sweet cherry for eating fresh or canning.

- Sam: Medium to large, firm, black fruit, ripens one week earlier than Bing.

- Stella: Large, nearly black, richly flavored sweet cherry. Similar to its parent, Lambert. Late harvest.

- Sunburst: Large, dark-skinned sweet cherry similar to Stella. Ripens midseason.

- Utah Giant: Best sweet cherry, according to Utah folks. Larger, firmer, more flavorful than Bing or Lambert. Good canner.

- Van: Fine fruit similar to Bing, though usually smaller.

Sour (Tart) Cherries

♦ Early Richmond: Early-ripening, flavorful, juicy, bright red fruit used primarily for cooking and canning. Sometimes used fresh when fully ripe. Origin unknown, planted in England in the early 1500s.

♦ Meteor Semi-Dwarf: Large, bright red fruit similar to Montmorency, used mostly for cooking. Tart, juicy, meaty flesh; colorless juice.

♦ Michigan Balaton: Larger, firmer, and significantly sweeter than the red tart cherries traditionally used in cherry pies with a deep, natural red pigment. These were recently introduced to the U.S. by Dr. Amy Iezzoni of Michigan State University but have grown for years in the towns and villages in Hungary.

♦ Montmorency: Large, light red skin, yellow flesh. Perfect for cobblers, pies, etc.

♦ North Star Dwarf: Large, meaty, tart, red-skinned fruit with red juice. Excellent for pies and cobblers, also used fresh when fully ripe.

♦ English Morello: Late-ripening tart cherry for cooking, sometimes eaten fresh when fully ripe. Dark red to nearly black fruit with dark juice.

Snacks
&
Appetizers

Jacquie Caters Cherry-Chevre Stuffed Dates

8 ounces cream cheese
4 ounces chevre (goat cheese)
$1/2$ cup dried cherries
8-ounce package pitted dates (32)
16 slices of bacon, cut in half

Equipment needed: pastry bag with medium round tip.

Place cream cheese, chevre and dried cherries in the bowl of food processor. Process until cheeses are well mixed, and cherries are finely chopped.

Preheat broiler.

Fill a pastry bag with the cheese mixture. Pipe the cheese mixture into the pitted dates until they are filled. You will have extra cheese mixture to use another time. Wrap the cheese stuffed dates with $1/2$ strip of bacon. Broil the dates on one side until the bacon is crisp. Turn the dates over and broil on the other side. Watch carefully, it only takes a few minutes. Let cool on paper towels for a few minutes. Serve with toothpicks.

Makes thirty-two appetizers

Jackie Cobb and Jacquie Honea of Jacquie Caters, Traverse City

Spicy Cherry Peanut Mix

2 cups lightly salted peanuts
1 cup dried cherries
2 tablespoons Worcestershire
$1/2$ teaspoon garlic powder
$1/2$ teaspoon seasoned salt
$1/2$ teaspoon ground cumin
$1/4$ teaspoon ground cayenne pepper
vegetable oil

Combine peanuts and cherries in a medium bowl. In a small bowl combine Worcestershire sauce, garlic powder, seasoned salt, cumin and cayenne pepper; mix well. Pour over peanut mixture; stir to coat.

Heat 1 or 2 teaspoons oil in large skillet over medium heat. Add peanut mixture. Cook for 3 or 4 minutes until peanuts are light brown. Remove from heat and spread on waxed paper or aluminum foil to cool. Store in a lightly covered container.

Cherry Marketing Institute

23

Firecracker Salsa

1/2 cup dried tart cherries
1/2 cup cherry, peach or raspberry jam
2 tablespoons red wine vinegar
1/2 cup red onion, chopped
1/2 yellow bell pepper, chopped
1/2 jalapeno pepper, chopped (add
 more or less to taste)
1 to 2 tablespoons cilantro, chopped
 fresh
juice of 1 lime

Combine dried cherries, preserves and vinegar in a small microwave-safe bowl; mix well. Microwave on High (100% power) 1 to $1^1/2$ minutes, or until hot. Let stand 5 minutes.

Stir in red onion, yellow bell pepper, jalapeno peppers, cilantro and lime juice. Refrigerate, covered, 3 to 4 hours or overnight. Serve with grilled swordfish or tuna. It's also excellent as a topping for hamburgers.

Makes about one and one half cups

Cherry Marketing Institute

Brie Torte

1 (15- to 16-ounce) wheel Brie cheese
$1/3$ cup butter, softened
$1/3$ cup chopped dried tart cherries
$1/4$ cup finely chopped pecans
$1/2$ teaspoon dried thyme
      (or 2 teaspoons finely
      chopped fresh thyme)

Crackers

Refrigerate Brie until chilled and firm; or freeze 30 minutes, or until firm. Cut Brie in half horizontally.

Combine butter, cherries, pecans and thyme in a small bowl; mix well. Evenly spread mixture on cut-side of one piece of the Brie. Top with the other piece, cut-side down. Lightly press together. Wrap in plastic wrap; refrigerate 1 to 2 hours. To serve, cut into serving-size wedges and bring to room temperature. Serve with crackers.

Note: If wrapped securely in plastic wrap, this appetizer will keep in the refrigerator for at least a week.

Makes about twenty servings

Cherry Marketing Institute

25

Crunchy Cherry Trail Mix

2 cups bite-size corn square cereal (Corn Chex)
2 cups bite-size rice square cereal (Rice Chex)
2 cups bite-size wheat square cereal (Wheat Chex)
2 cups broken whole wheat Melba toast
2 cups small fat-free pretzel twists
3 tablespoons margarine or butter, melted
1 tablespoon Worcestershire sauce
2 teaspoons chili powder
1/4 teaspoon onion powder
1/8 teaspoons ground red pepper
1 1/2 cups dried tart cherries

Preheat oven to 300 degrees.

Put cereals, melba toast, and pretzels in a large bowl; stir to mix. In a measuring cup or small bowl, stir together the melted butter or margarine, Worcestershire sauce, chili powder, garlic powder, onion powder, and ground red pepper. Drizzle over cereal mixture.

Spread cereal mixture in a 15 x 10 x 1-inch (or 13 x 9 x 2 inch) baking pan. Bake for about 25 minutes, stirring every 7 to 8 minutes. Remove from oven; stir in dried cherries. Let cook completely. Store in a tightly covered container for up to 1 week.

Makes twenty servings

Cherry Marketing Institute

26

Jacquie Caters Nutty Cherry Gorgonzola Balls

2 tablespoons butter
$3/4$ cup walnuts, finely chopped
8 ounces cream cheese
4 ounces Gorgonzola cheese
$1/2$ cup dried cherries

Melt butter in a sauté pan over medium-high heat. Sauté walnuts until lightly browned and fragrant. Place cream cheese, Gorgonzola and cherries in the bowl of your food processor until the mixture is creamy and the cherries are finely chopped. Transfer mixture into a bowl and place in the freezer for 30 minutes.

Take the chilled mixture out of the freezer and scoop and mold into walnut-sized balls. Roll the ball of cheese in the butter-toasted walnuts until covered. Place the mini-cheese balls in a container and chill at least 4 hours to blend flavors.

When ready to serve, cut the balls in half with a serrated knife, using a sawing motion. Serve on crackers, toasted baguettes, or with apple or pear slices.

Serves eight to twelve

Jackie Cobb and Jacquie Honea , Jacquie Caters, Traverse City, Michigan

Bob's Great Cocktail Meatballs

meatballs:
1 pound ground beef
$1/2$ cup dry bread crumbs
$1/3$ cup onion, finely chopped
$1/4$ cup milk
1 egg
2 tablespoons dried parsley
1 teaspoon Worcestershire sauce
$1/4$ teaspoon salt
dash of black pepper

sauce:
1 cup ketchup
1 jar cherry pepper jam or cherry jam
$1/2$ cup dried cherries

Mix together ground beef, bread crumbs, onion, milk, egg, parsley, Worcestershire sauce, salt, and pepper. Shape into 1-inch balls.

Brown meatballs in a large nonstick skillet over medium heat until done. Remove meatballs from the skillet. Remove and discard any fat from the skillet. Heat ketchup and cherry jam in the skillet, stirring until blended.

Add dried cherries to the sauce mixture. Add meatballs and stir until coated with sauce. Simmer uncovered 30 minutes, stirring occasionally.

Makes thirty to forty meatballs

Bob Lange, Cherry Stop, downtown Traverse City, Michigan

Veggie Dip

1 cup dried tart cherries, chopped
$1/2$ cup crumbled blue cheese
$1/2$ cup chopped walnuts
1 cup sour cream
$1/4$ cup mayonnaise

Combine cherries, blue cheese and walnuts in a medium bowl. Stir in sour cream and mayonnaise; mix well. Chill about 1 hour to blend flavors. Serve with vegetable dippers, (carrots sticks, celery, broccoli, green peppers) or with crackers.

Serves twenty-four

Cherry Marketing Institute

Daystarters

Russian Walnut-Cherry Latkes with Cherry-Apple Sauce

$1/_4$ cup dried tart cherries

1 7.5-ounce package farmer's cheese, drained

2 tablespoons cream cheese, room temperature

4 large eggs, separated

1 teaspoon vanilla extract

5 tablespoons all purpose flour

2 tablespoons (packed) golden brown sugar

$1/_4$ teaspoon salt

$1/_3$ cup finely chopped lightly toasted walnuts

3 tablespoons (about) unsalted butter

3 tablespoons (about) vegetable oil

Cherry-Apple Sauce on following page

Place cherries in small bowl with enough hot water to cover; soak until plumped, about 10 minutes. Drain. Set aside.

Blend both cheeses, egg yolks, and vanilla extract in processor just until smooth, about 30 seconds. Add flour, sugar, and salt and mix in, using on/off turns, just until blended. Transfer batter to large bowl. Mix in reserved cherries and chopped walnuts.

Using electric mixer, beat egg whites in large bowl until stiff but not dry. Gently fold whites into batter in 3 additions.

Melt 1 tablespoon butter with 1 tablespoon oil in heavy large nonstick skillet over medium heat until hot but not smoking. Working in batches, drop batter by heaping tablespoonfuls into skillet and spread to $2^1/_2$-inch rounds. Cook until bottoms are golden, about $1^1/2$ minutes per side. Using slotted spatula, transfer latkes to plates. Add more butter and oil as necessary and allow to get hot before adding more batter. Serve immediately with Cherry-Apple Sauce.

Makes about sixteen

Cherry-Apple Sauce

5 Gala or Golden Delicious apples
    (about 2 pounds), peeled,
    cored, and cut into $1/_2$-inch
    pieces
$1/_4$ cup unsweetened apple juice
$1/_4$ cup cherry preserves

Combine apple pieces and unsweetened apple juice in heavy large saucepan. Bring to a boil, stirring occasionally. Cover, reduce heat to low and simmer occasionally, about 15 minutes. Remove from heat. Mix in cherry preserves. Using a potato masher or fork, mash mixture to chunky puree. (Sauce can be prepared up to 2 days ahead. Cover and refrigerate.)

Serve hot or cold.

Bon Appetit December 2001

Wholesome Granola Bars

$1^1/_2$ cups low-fat plain granola
1 cup quick-cooking oatmeal
$^3/_4$ cup dried tart cherries
$^1/_2$ cup whole wheat flour
$^1/_3$ cup slivered almonds, toasted
$^1/_2$ teaspoon ground cinnamon
2 beaten egg whites
$^1/_3$ cup honey
$^1/_4$ cup brown sugar, firmly packed
2 tablespoons vegetable oil

Line bottom and sides of an 8 x 8 x 2 -inch baking pan with foil. Lightly spray the foil with non-stick cooking spray. Set aside. Combine granola, oatmeal, cherries, whole wheat flour, almonds, and cinnamon in a large mixing bowl. Stir together egg white, honey, brown sugar and oil. Stir into the granola mixture, mix until all ingredients are coated. Press mixture evenly into the prepared pan. Bake for 20 to 25 minutes, or until light brown. Let cool on a wire rack. Use foil to remove from pan. Let cool completely. Cut into bars.

Makes twenty bars

Cherry Marketing Institute

Michigan Baked Oatmeal

2 cups old fashioned oatmeal
4 cups milk
$1/2$ teaspoon cinnamon
$1/4$ cup brown sugar
$1/2$ cup walnuts, chopped
$1/2$ cup dried cherries
1 large apple unpeeled, grated

Preheat oven to 400 degrees.

Coat 3 quart casserole or baking pan with cooking spray. In mixing bowl, combine all ingredients. Transfer to baking dish. Sprinkle top with additional almonds.

Bake uncovered for 45 minutes. Serve hot.

Serves six to eight

Stuffed Apple with Maple Sauce

³/4 cup dried cherries
³/4 cup brown sugar
¹/4 cup chopped walnuts
1 teaspoon cinnamon
¹/2 teaspoon nutmeg
8 baking apples
1 cup apple juice
¹/2 cup maple syrup
1 tablespoon butter

Preheat oven to 350 degrees.

Combine cherries, brown sugar, walnuts and spices in a small bowl. Core apples $3/4$ of the way through. Peel top half of each apple. Fill apples with mixture. Place apples in a heavy oven-proof skillet. Add juice to skillet. Combine maple syrup and butter and pour over apples. Bake covered for 20 minutes. Uncover, baste with juices from the skillet and bake an additional 20 minutes.

Serves eight

Cherry Marketing Institute

UP into the cherry tree
Who should climb but little me?
I held the trunk with both my hands
And looked abroad on foreign land.

I saw the next door garden lie,
Adorned with flowers, before my eye,
And many pleasant places more
That I had never see before.

If I could find a higher tree
Farther and farther I should see
To where the grown-up river slips
Into the sea among the ships,

To where the roads on either hand
Lead onward into fairy land,
Where all the children dine at five,
And all the playthings come alive.

Foreign Lands. Robert Louis Stevenson.
A Child's Garden of Verses and Underwoods. 1913

Cherry Pancakes

Pancake batter:
2 cups flour
5 teaspoons baking powder
2 teaspoons salt
3 tablespoons sugar
2 eggs
2 cups milk
6 tablespoons oil
3/4 cup dried cherries

Cherry syrup:
1 cup cherry juice
1 tablespoon cornstarch
1/2 teaspoon salt
1 tablespoon butter

Heat griddle:

For pancakes:
Mix dry ingredients and stir in eggs, milk and oil until just blended. Pour batter onto a hot griddle. Drop a few dried cherries on each pancake. Turn cakes when bubbles form and edges brown. Serve with cherry or maple syrup.

For cherry syrup:
Combine ingredients in saucepan and cook over medium heat until thickened.

Serves six

Rich Travis' Cherry Mascarpone French Toast

1 loaf white bread, cut into cubes
4 cups frozen cherries, rinsed and
    drained
16 ounces Mascarpone cheese,
    softened
1 cup sugar, divided
2 teaspoons vanilla, divided
$1/2$ cup sour cream
$1/2$ loaf French bread
7 eggs
$1^1/2$ cups milk
$1^1/2$ cups half & half
$1/4$ cup powdered sugar
1 cup sliced almonds

Place cubes of white bread into a greased 9 x 13-inch pan. Spread cherries over the bread. Add $1/2$ cup sugar, 1 teaspoon of the vanilla and sour cream to cheese. Spread over the cherries. Cut ten 1-inch-thick slices of French bread. Place the slices over the cheese mixture. In a small bowl, beat the eggs well and add the remaining $1/2$ cup sugar, 1 teaspoon of vanilla, milk, and half & half and beat again. Pour egg mixture over French bread slices. Cover and refrigerate over-night.

Preheat oven to 350 degrees. Bake covered with tin foil for 40-50 minutes and uncover for last 10 minutes or so to brown slightly. Let rest for 10 minutes. Sprinkle top with powdered sugar and sliced almonds before cutting.

Serves ten

Richard Travis, executive chef of Latitude Restaurant, Bay Harbor, MI

Peachy's Cherry Breakfast Bread Pudding

1 pound bread
$1/2$ cup butter, melted
$1/4$ cup sugar
1 tablespoon cinnamon
1 cup dried cherries
3 cups half & half
$1/2$ cup brown sugar
6 eggs, slightly beaten
dash of salt

Preheat oven to 350 degrees.

Cube the bread and toss with the melted butter. Stir the sugar and cinnamon together and toss with bread. Place in a buttered 9 x 13-inch baking pan. Sprinkle with dried cherries. Stir together half & half, brown sugar, eggs, and salt. Pour egg mixture over bread. Bake for 35 to 40 minutes or until set. Serve with syrup.

May be made the night before and refrigerated until the morning before baking.

Serves eight

La Bécasse, Burdickville, Michigan near Glen Lake

Nickerson Inn's Cherry Banana Loaf

4 tablespoons butter
1 1/2 teaspoons each cinnamon and
    sugar, mixed
2 small very ripe bananas
1 large egg
2/3 cup sugar
1 pinch salt
1 1/4 cups all-purpose flour
1 teaspoon baking soda
1 tablespoon dark molasses
1/3 cup pitted or dried tart **cherries**,
    chopped

Preheat the oven to 375 degrees.

Grease a 9x5x3-inch loaf pan with a small amount of the butter and dust with the cinnamon and sugar mixture. Beat the bananas, butter, egg, sugar and salt with an electric mixer at medium speed to blend, then add the flour, baking soda and molasses and blend until all ingredients are thoroughly mixed. Stir in cherries. Pour into the greased loaf pan and bake at 375 degrees for 45 minutes.

Remove from oven, cool slightly in the pan, then turn onto a wire rack to cool. Flavors are best after a day or two.

Makes one loaf.

Nickerson Inn, Pentwater, MI

Cherry Almond Bubble Bread

1 3/4 cup firmly packed brown sugar, divided

2 teaspoons cinnamon

3 10-biscuit cans of refrigerated biscuits

1/2 cup dried cherries, divided

1/4 cup sliced almonds, divided

1/2 cup butter

Preheat oven to 350 degrees.

Grease a bundt pan. Combine 3/4 cup brown sugar and cinnamon in plastic bag. Separate biscuit dough and cut into quarters. Toss biscuit pieces with sugar/cinnamon mixture until well coated.

Arrange layer of 1/3 of the biscuit pieces in pan; sprinkle with 1/3 cherries and 1/3 almonds. Repeat layers 2 times.

Melt butter with 1 cup brown sugar. Boil for exactly 1 minute. Pour over biscuit pieces. Bake for 25 to 30 minutes or until golden brown. Cool in pan 5 to 10 minutes before turning out onto serving platter. Cut into 1/2-inch slices.

Serves twelve

Bountiful Arbor

Cherry Oatmeal Muffins

1 cup old-fashioned or
    quick-cooking oats,
    uncooked
1 cup all-purpose flour
$1/2$ cup brown sugar, firmly packed
$1^1/2$ teapoon baking powder
$1/4$ teaspoon ground nutmeg
$3/4$ cup buttermilk
1 egg, slightly beaten
$1/4$ cup vegetable oil
1 teaspoon almond extract
1 cup frozen tart cherries, coarsely
    chopped

Put oats, flour, brown sugar, baking powder and nutmeg in a large mixing bowl; mix well.

Combine buttermilk, egg, oil and almond extract in a small bowl. Pour buttermilk mixture into oats mixture; stir just to moisten ingredients. Quickly stir in cherries. (It is not necessary to thaw cherries before chopping and adding to batter.)

Spray muffin pan with non-stick spray. Fill muffin cups two-thirds full. Bake for 15 to 20 minutes of until a toothpick inserted in the center of a cupcake comes out clean.

Makes twelve muffins

Cherry Marketing Institute

Dried Cherry Scones

2^1/$_2$ cups flour
2 teaspoons baking powder
pinch of salt
3 tablespoons butter, room
    temperature
5 teaspoons sugar
^{1}/$_3$ cup dried **cherries**
1 large egg, lightly beaten
^{1}/$_2$ cup plus 1 teaspoon milk
clotted cream (optional)
strawberry jam (optional)

Preheat oven to 425 degrees.

Grease a baking sheet. Sift together flour, baking powder, and salt. Cut in butter until mixture resembles breadcrumbs, then stir in sugar and cherries. Add egg and ^{1}/$_2$ cup milk. Mix lightly until dough forms. On a lightly floured surface, roll dough to ^{3}/$_4$ inch thick. Using a 2 ^{1}/$_4$-inch biscuit cutter, cut rounds, rerolling the dough as necessary. Place scones on baking sheet and brush tops with 1 teaspoon milk.

Bake for 12 to 15 minutes until golden. Serve warm with clotted cream and strawberry jam.

Makes ten scones

Bountiful Arbor

Cherry Island Muffins

2 cups all-purpose flour
$1/2$ cup firmly packed brown sugar
$1/2$ cup toasted wheat germ
2 teaspoons baking powder
1 teaspoon baking soda
1 cup coarsely chopped fresh **cherries**
  or frozen, thawed and
  drained
$1/3$ cup granulated sugar
$3/4$ cup orange juice
$1/3$ cup vegetable oil
1 egg, slightly beaten
$11/2$ teaspoons grated orange peel
1 teaspoon vanilla extract
$1/2$ cup chopped pecans

Preheat oven to 400 degrees.

Grease 12 muffin cups. In a large bowl, stir together the flour, brown sugar, wheat germ, baking powder and baking soda. In a small bowl, stir the cherries and sugar together. In a medium bowl, stir together the orange juice, oil, egg, orange peel and vanilla until blended.

Make a well in the center of the dry ingredients; add the cherry mixture and stir just to combine. Do not overmix. Fold in the pecans. Spoon batter into muffin cups, filling them $2/3$ full. Bake 15 to 20 minutes or until a cake tester inserted in the center of a muffin comes out clean. Cool 5 minutes on a wire rack before removing from muffin cups.

Makes twelve muffins

Michigan Balaton Cherry Focaccia

Dough:

1^1/2 cups warm water

2 tablespoons yeast

^{1}/2 cup sugar

2 teaspoons salt

2 teaspoons vanilla

^{1}/2 teaspoon mahlep powder (or almond extract)

2 eggs

^{1}/2 cup unsalted butter - melted

5 to 6 cups bread flour

Topping:

^{1}/3 cup unsalted butter - melted

^{1}/2 cup sugar

1 to 2 teaspoons cinnamon

2 cups fresh (or frozen) pitted Balaton **cherries** - or a mix ture of tart and sweet cherries (halved and whole). See re source page to order Balaton cherries by mail.

*Mahlep powder is a Turkish seasoning made from ground cherry pit centers. It boosts the flavor. Look for mahlep in Middle Eastern food stores.

Preheat oven to 350 degrees.

In a large bowl or in the bowl of an electric mixer fitted with a dough hook, whisk together water and yeast. Let stand a few minutes then stir in sugar, salt, vanilla, mahlep powder (almond extract), eggs, butter and most of flour. Stir until you have a soft mass. Knead for 8 to 10 minutes to form a soft dough (adding more flour as required). Form dough into a ball and place it in a well greased bowl. Cover, and allow to rise for 45 to 60 minutes.

Line a large baking sheet with parchment paper. When dough has risen, gently deflate and flatten to fit sheet. If it springs back, let it rest a moment then coax to fit sheet. Insert entire sheet in a large plastic bag. Let rise 30 minutes.

Generously brush dough with the melted butter. Generously dust with sugar and cinnamon and then scatter cherries on top. Bake until done (bread is golden, cherries are softened and oozing) about 45 to 55 minutes. Cut into slabs to serve.

Serves ten to twelve

www.betterbaking.com

Ric Bohy's Soda Bread
with Michigan Cherries and Toasted Pine Nuts

4 cups unbleached all-purpose flour
    (King Arthur brand is
    excellent)

1 teaspoon baking soda

1 teaspoon baking powder

1 teaspoon salt

1/2 stick (4 tablespoons) unsalted
    butter, softened but not melted

1 cup dried Michigan tart cherries

1/2 cup pine nuts, toasted (see note
    below)

1 1/2 cups room temperature
    buttermilk

1/4 cup honey (preferably clover,
    orange blossom or chestnut)

1 egg

2 tablespoons milk

Raw sugar, or Demerara sugar, for
    sprinkling

Note: To toast pine nuts, spread them in a single layer in a dry non-stick pan and stir gently over medium heat until brown and fragrant.

Preheat oven to 350.

Grease and flour a cookie sheet. Sift together flour, baking soda, baking powder and salt. Add butter. Using your fingers, rub butter together with dry ingredients until the mixture looks like moist meal or crumbs. Stir in dried cherries and pine nuts. In another bowl, stir together buttermilk and honey until well blended, then add to flour mixture and stir until just mixed.

Turn the dough out onto a well-floured surface and knead for a minute or two until relatively smooth. Cut dough in half, shape each piece into a round loaf, and place both – well spaced – on the prepared cookie sheet. Using a razor blade or very sharp knife, slash an "X" or "#" into the surface of each loaf. Beat together egg and milk to make a glaze, and brush it evenly over the surface of each loaf. Sprinkle with sugar. Let loaves rest for 15 minutes.

Bake for 40 minutes, until loaves sound hollow when tapped on the bottom. Cool on racks before serving.

Makes two round loaves

Ric Bohy, editor and chief food and restaurant critic of *HOUR DETROIT* magazine.

Big Cherries
Postcard by Orson W. Peck, Traverse City, Michigan, obviously doctored
size of cherries in foreground!

Cherry Orange Poppy Seed Muffins

2 cups all-purpose flour
$1/2$ cup Miller's bran
$3/4$ cup granulated sugar
1 tablespoon poppy seeds
1 tablespoon baking powder
$1/4$ teaspoon salt
1 cup milk
$1/4$ cup ($1/2$ stick) butter, melted
1 egg, slightly beaten
$1/2$ cup dried tart cherries
3 tablespoons grated orange peel

Preheat oven to 400 degrees.

Combine flour, Miller's bran, sugar, poppy seeds, baking powder and salt in a large mixing bowl. Add milk, melted butter and egg, stirring just until dry ingredients are moistened. Gently stir in cherries and orange peel. Fill paper-lined muffin cups $3/4$ full.

Bake for 18 to 22 minutes, or until wooden pick inserted in center comes out clean. Let cool in pan 5 minutes. Remove from pan and serve warm or let cool completely.

Makes eighteen muffins

Cherry Marketing Institute

Cherry Hearth Bread

1 cup buttermilk
$^1/_2$ cup water
$^1/_2$ cup apple cider or apple juice
$^1/_4$ cup honey
2 scant tablespoons yeast
2 scant tablespoons salt
5 cups bread flour
2 $^1/_2$ cups whole wheat flour
2 $^1/_2$ teaspoons cinnamon
1 cup dried cherries, chopped
1 cup walnuts, chopped

Preheat oven to 400 degrees.

Combine liquid ingredients in a large bowl. Add honey and yeast and stir until combined. Let set until yeast is bloomed - about 15 minutes. Add remaining ingredients and stir until a stiff dough is formed. Turn onto a lightly floured board and knead for 8 to 10 minutes. Return to the bowl and set in a warm place to rise until double (about 1 hour).

Punch down and divide into two pieces. Round into balls and let rise until almost double. Place in oven and bake until golden brown.

Makes two rounds

Northwestern Michigan College Culinary Arts Department

Cherry Zucchini Bread

2 eggs
$3/4$ cup granulated sugar
$1/3$ cup vegetable oil
$1/3$ cup lemon juice
$1/4$ cup water
2 cups all-purpose flour
2 teaspoons baking powder
1 teaspoon ground cinnamon
$1/2$ teaspoon baking soda
$1/4$ teaspoon salt
$2/3$ cup zucchini, unpeeled, shredded
$2/3$ cup dried tart cherries
1 tablespoon lemon peel, grated

Preheat oven to 350 degrees.

Put eggs in a large mixing bowl. Beat with an electric mixer on medium speed 3 to 4 minutes, or until eggs are thick and lemon colored. Add sugar, oil, lemon juice and water; mix well. Combine flour, baking powder, cinnamon, soda and salt. Add flour mixture to egg mixture; mix well. Stir in zucchini. Grease and flour the bottom only of an $8^1/2$ x $4^1/2$-inch loaf pan. Pour batter into prepared pan.

Bake in oven for 55 to 65 minutes or until wooden pick inserted in center comes out clean. Let cool in pan on wire rack 10 minutes. Loosen edges with a metal spatula. Remove from pan. Let cool completely. Wrap tightly in plastic wrap and store in refrigerator.

Makes one loaf, about sixteen slices

Cherry Marketing Institute

Cherry Yogurt Bread for Bread Machine

REGULAR (1-pound loaf)
$1/2$ cup water
2 cups white bread flour
$3/4$ teaspoon salt
$1/2$ cup **cherries**, dried
$1/3$ cup cherry yogurt, low fat
2 tablespoons applesauce,
         unsweetened
2 teaspoons brown sugar
$1^1/2$ teaspoons fast rise yeast OR
2 teaspoons active dry yeast

LARGE (1 $1/2$- pound loaf)
$3/4$ cup water
3 cups white bread flour
1 $1/4$ teaspoons salt
$3/4$ cup **cherries**, dried
$1/2$ cup cherry yogurt
$1/4$ cup applesauce, unsweetened
1 tablespoon brown sugar
2 teaspoons fastrise yeast OR
         3 teaspoons active dry yeast

Add ingredients in the correct order for your bread machine. Use low fat fruited yogurt.

Add the dry cherries whole. If you want whole cherries, add them at the beep in the fruit/nut cycle. This recipe can be used with the regular and rapid bake cycles. If using the rapid bake cycle, add cherries and walnuts with other ingredients.

Makes one eight-slice loaf

Cherry-Nut Bread for Bread Machine

REGULAR (1-pound loaf)

3/4 cup water

2 cups white bread flour

1 tablespoon dry milk

1 tablespoon sugar

1 teaspoon salt

1 tablespoon butter

1/2 teaspoon cinnamon

1/2 cup **cherries**, dried

1/4 cup walnuts, toasted

1 1/2 teaspoons fast rise yeast OR

      2 teaspoons active dry yeast

LARGE (1 1/2-pound loaf)

1 1/4 cups water

3 cups white bread flour

2 tablespoons dry milk

1 1/2 teaspoons sugar

1 1/2 teaspoons salt

2 tablespoons butter

1 teaspoon cinnamon

1 cup **cherries**, dried

1/2 cup walnuts, toasted

3 teaspoons fastrise yeast OR

      3 teaspoons active dry yeast

Add ingredients in the correct order for your bread machine.

Add the dry cherries whole. If you want whole cherries, add them at the beep in the fruit/nut cycle. This recipe can be used with the regular and rapid bake cycles. If using the rapid bake cycle, add cherries and walnuts with other ingredients.

Makes one eight-slice loaf

Salads
&
Sides and Sauces

Patty's Zippy Broccoli Cherry Salad

4 cups broccoli florets, rinsed and
    drained
1/4 cup dried tart **cherries**
1/4 medium red onion, sliced thin
1/4-pound lean maple-cured bacon, in
    bite-size pieces, cooked and
    drained on paper towels
1/4 cup sour cream
2 tablespoons prepared horseradish
2 tablespoons mayonnaise
Salt and pepper to taste

In a four-quart pot of salted boiling water, blanch the broccoli florets until bright green, and then drain in a colander.

In a large bowl, combine the broccoli, cherries, onion and cooked bacon.

In a small bowl, combine the sour cream, horse-radish, and mayonnaise and mix well. Pour dressing over the broccoli salad and toss until all ingredients are well coated.

Refrigerate, covered, until ready to serve.

Serves six

Patty LaNoue Stearns

Wild Rice and Cherry Pilaf

$3/4$ cup wild rice, rinsed

3 cups chicken broth

$1/2$ cup pearl barley

$1/4$ cup snipped dried **cherries**

1 tablespoon butter

$1/3$ cup sliced almonds, toasted

Preheat oven to 325 degrees

In a saucepan combine rice and chicken broth. Bring to a boil; reduce heat. Stir in barley, cherries, and butter. Spoon into a $1^1/2$-quart casserole.

Bake, covered, for 55 to 60 minutes or until rice and barley are tender and liquid is absorbed, stirring once. Fluff rice mixture with a fork; stir in almonds.

Serves twelve

Adapted from *Bountiful Arbor*

Spinach with Pine Nuts and Cherries

3 tablespoons extra virgin olive oil

$1/2$ onion, chopped

2 cloves of garlic, sliced

2 bunches spinach, fresh, washed,
    trimmed

3 tablespoons pine nuts, toasted

1 teaspoon lemon juice

8 strips lemon zest, thin

$1/4$ to $1/2$ cup dried **cherries**

Heat olive oil in a large skillet.

Add onion and garlic and cook over medium heat until soft, about 5 minutes. Add spinach and cook, stirring for 1 minute. Cover and cook, stirring until wilted, 2 to 3 minutes.

Add pine nuts, lemon juice, lemon zest, and cherries. Season to taste with salt and pepper.

Serves four

Jimmy Schmidt's Radicchio, Mâche and Dried Cherry Salad

1/4 cup red wine vinegar
1/4 cup dried **cherries**
2 tablespoons shallots, finely diced
salt to taste
1/2 cup extra virgin olive oil
black pepper to taste, coarsely ground
1 head radicchio, trimmed
4 bunches mâche, stemmed
2 tablespoons snipped fresh chives,
        cut into 1-inch lengths
1/2 cup crumbled Roquefort or blue
        cheese (optional)

In a small saucepan, heat the vinegar, then add the cherries. Remove from heat and allow to steep until softened, at least 2 hours. (Add a little water if the cherries are still firm.)

Place the vinegar, cherries, and shallots in a blender and puree until smooth. While the machine is running, add olive oil until thickened, then add salt and pepper.

Carefully peel off the leaves from the head of radicchio. Select four of the best large leaves and place in the centers of the serving plates. Cut the remaining leaves into 1/4-inch chiffonade.
In a medium-size bowl, combine the chiffonaded radicchio and the mâche leaves.

Add the dressing and toss. Arrange the tossed greens on the large radicchio leaves. Sprinkle with the chives and blue cheese and serve.

Serves four

Butter Lettuce Salad
with Bacon and Roquefort Vinaigrette

Salad:
8 slices bacon, diced
2 large heads of butter lettuce
$1/2$ cup dried cherries

Vinaigrette:
3 tablespoons mayonnaise
2 tablespoons white wine vinegar
$1/2$ cup vegetable oil
1 cup crumbled Roquefort cheese
salt and pepper, to taste

Saute' bacon in heavy medium skillet over medium-high heat until brown and crisp. Using slotted spoon, transfer bacon to paper-towel-lined plate to drain. Set aside.

Tear lettuce into bite-size pieces and toss with half of cherries and half of bacon and with enough dressing to coat. Divide salad among 6 plates. Top with remaining cherries and bacon.

Vinaigrette:
Whisk mayonnaise and vinegar in medium bowl. Gradually whisk in oil, then cheese. Season vinaigrette with salt and pepper.

Serves six

Bon Appetit December 2001

Cranberry Sauce
with Cherries, Marsala and Rosemary

2 cups dry Marsala
$1/2$ cup dried tart cherries
1 12-ounce bag cranberries
12 ounces frozen dark sweet cherries
      (about 2 $2/3$ cups), halved
1 cup (packed) golden brown sugar
1 teaspoon minced fresh rosemary
$1/2$ teaspoon ground allspice

Combine Marsala and dried cherries in deep saucepan.

Boil until mixture is reduced to $2/3$ cup, about 8 minutes. Mix in remaining ingredients. Bring to boil, stirring occasionally. Reduce heat to medium, cover pan and simmer until cranberries burst and mixture thickens, stirring occasionally, about 8 minutes.

Transfer to bowl. Refrigerate until cold, about 3 hours. (Can be prepared 1 week ahead. Cover; keep refrigerated.)

Bon Appétit November 1999

Cherry Sunflower Salad

1 bunch (about 1 pound) broccoli,
    rinsed and cut into bite-size
    pieces
1 1/2 cups shredded Cheddar or
    Monterey Jack cheese
5 to 6 strips bacon, fried crisp and
    crumbled
1 cup dried cherries
3/4 cup shelled sunflower seeds
1/2 cup chopped onion
1/2 cup mayonnaise
1/2 cup plain yogurt
2 tablespoons Cherry Wine Vinegar
    (or substitute red wine
    vinegar)

In a large mixing bowl, combine broccoli, cheese, bacon, cherries, sunflower seeds and onion; mix well.

In a small container, combine mayonnaise, yogurt and vinegar; mix well. Pour mayonnaise mixture over broccoli mixture; toss to coat all ingredients.

Refrigerate until ready to serve.

Serves six

Cherry Marketing Institute

Leelanau Country Inn's Salad Leelanau

Salad:
1 head bibb lettuce, large
1 head red Boston bibb, large
4 tablespoons pecans, chopped and
    toasted
4 tablespoons Gorgonzola cheese
3 tablespoons dried cherries
1/2 cup cherry vinaigrette dressing

Cherry Vinaigrette Dressing:
1 cup cherry vinegar
2 cups canola oil
1 cup maple syrup
1/4 cup country Dijon mustard
1/4 cup basil, fresh, chopped

For salad:
Prepare pecans by chopping and then under a hot broiler, toast for 2 minutes or until golden brown. Chill large salad bowl. Wash and dry the lettuces*. Hand-tear the lettuces into the large salad bowl, and mix well. Sprinkle pecans, cheese, and dried cherries on the lettuces. At the table, before serving, toss with Cherry Vinaigrette Dressing.

*Note: Dressing will not stick to wet lettuce. Always be certain the lettuce is dry by draining for several hours or spinning dry, and carefully patting with a dry towel.

For dressing:
Mix all ingredients together well. May be stored, sealed under refrigeration for up to 1 month. It is always best to make dressing at least one day ahead of use to allow the flavors to marry. Cherry vinegar is available in most speciality shops. To make your own, combine 2 cups white vinegar and 2 cups red wine vinegar and add 3 cups of tart cherries cut in half. Allow to stand for 36 hours. Then strain.

Serves four

Leelanau Country Inn Cookery...Continued

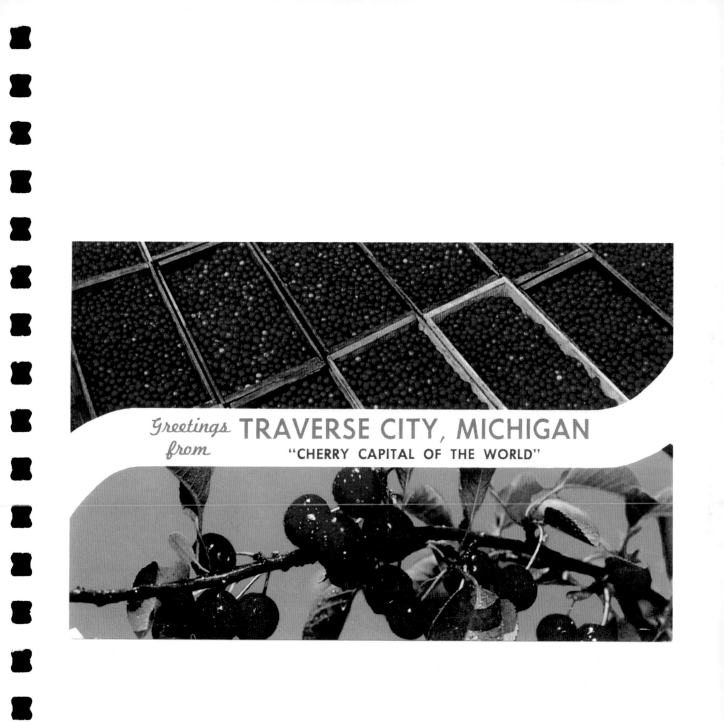

Greetings from **TRAVERSE CITY, MICHIGAN**
"CHERRY CAPITAL OF THE WORLD"

Jon Eakes' Dried Cherry Sauce for Duck

2 cups chicken stock
6 cups veal stock
2 tablespoons shallot, freshly minced
24 fluid ounces (2 bottles) beer, Bell's
    Oberon
2 cups dried cherries
2 teaspoons thyme, whole leaf
2 tablespoons cornstarch
8 tablespoons water
1 teaspoon salt
1 teaspoon pepper, freshly cracked

Combine stocks in 4-quart saucepan. Add beer, shallots and thyme. Simmer for 15 minutes until alcohol has evaporated from the beer.

Add dried cherries and check seasonings. Slurry to thicken with cornstarch and water. Salt and pepper to taste. Hold or serve.

La Cuisine Amical, Traverse City

Nickerson Inn's Cherry Chipotle Chutney

1 large yellow onion, diced
2 large Delicious apples, cored and
    diced with skin on
1 tablespoon canola or vegetable oil
1 tablespoon butter, melted
1 cup sugar
4 tablespoons cider vinegar
2 teaspoons orange zest
1 teaspoon chipotle pepper, diced
1 teaspoon cinnamon
$1/2$ teaspoon dry mustard
$1/4$ teaspoon ground ginger
pinch of salt
2 cups chicken stock
4 cups dried tart cherries

Saute' onions and apples in the oil and butter until light brown. Add remaining ingredients except cherries and simmer for 5 minutes. Add cherries and continue until liquid is reduced by half. Serve on pork, chicken, or grilled salmon. Try topping the chutney on brie and serve with crackers.

Serves six

Nickerson Inn, Pentwater, Michigan

Keil Moshier's Fall Fruit Chutney

1/4 cup red onion, diced small
1 quart apple cider vinegar
1 pound brown sugar
1 pound sliced peaches
2 cups tart pitted cherries (with some
    juice)
2 cups sliced apples (with some
    juice)
1 cup dried cherries
1/2 cup dried cranberries

Mix all ingredients in a large saucepot and bring to a boil. Reduce the heat to a simmer and cook until it has reduced by one-third. Stir very often to keep from burning. Allow to cool overnight in the refrigerator before using.

Serves four to six

Keil Moshier, executive chef, Bowers Harbor Inn, Old Mission Peninsula, Traverse City, Michigan

Dried Cherry and Shallot Confit

$1^1/2$ cups dried sour cherries
$1/2$ cup white-wine vinegar
$1/4$ cup balsamic vinegar
2 cups thinly sliced shallot
1 cup finely chopped onion
2 tablespoons unsalted butter
3 tablespoons sugar

In a bowl let the cherries soak in the vinegars for 30 minutes. While the cherries are soaking, in a heavy skillet, cook the shallot and the onion in the butter, covered, over moderately low heat, stirring occasionally, for 10 minutes, or until the shallot is soft.

Sprinkle mixture with the sugar and cook the mixture, covered, stirring occasionally, for 10 minutes.

Add the cherries with the soaking liquid, simmer the mixture, uncovered, for 10 to 15 minutes, or until almost all the liquid is evaporated, and season the confit with salt and pepper.

The confit may be made 1 day in advance, kept covered and chilled, and reheated.

Makes about two cups.

Gourmet October 1991

Kate Lawson's Brown Rice Salad with Cherries

1 cup mixed brown rice (I use the
    Lundberg mix with wild,
    brown, etc.)
1/3 cup fresh or dried **cherries**,
    pitted
1/2 cup brandy
3 tablespoons balsamic or Sherry
    vinegar
3 tablespoons extra virgin olive oil
Kosher salt to taste
Freshly ground black pepper to taste
3/4 cup chopped pecans or almonds,
    toasted
1 bunch green onions, chopped (use
    some green parts, too)
1 small yellow or orange bell pepper,
    chopped small
1 ripe pear, peeled, cored and
    chopped small

Cook rice according to package directions. While rice is cooking, place cherries and brandy in small saucepan, bring to boil, cover and remove from heat. Let steep while rice is cooking. Then drain.

Make vinaigrette by whisking together vinegar, olive oil, salt and pepper in a small bowl.

When rice is cooked, stir in cherries, nuts, pear and vegetables. Pour in vinaigrette and stir gently.

Let sit for 1 hour at room temperature before serving.

Serves six

Kate Lawson, *Detroit News* food columnist

Nancy Stuck's Cherry Ramen Noodle Salad

1 package shredded cabbage
3 green onions, rinsed and chopped
$^1/_4$ cup sunflower seeds
1 cup slivered almonds
$^1/_4$ cup sesame seeds
1 red pepper, rinsed and slivered
1 small package slivered carrots
$^1/_2$ cup dried cherries
2 packages chicken Ramen noodles,
    uncooked and broken up

Dressing:
1 cup peanut or canola oil
6 tablespoons cherry vinegar (or any
    other vinegar)
1 teaspoon pepper
2 tablespoons sugar
$^1/_2$ teaspoon red pepper
2 chicken-flavored packets from
    Ramen noodles

Assemble the salad ingredients in a large mixing bowl. Top with dressing; mix well and serve.

Serves six

Nancy Stuck is an artist in Traverse City

Sylvia Rector's Cherry Wild Rice Salad

1/2 cup dried cherries

1/2 cup dried apricots, cut in matchstick julienne

1 cup orange juice

1 cup uncooked wild rice, rinsed and drained

5 1/2 cups chicken broth

1 cup pecan halves, lightly toasted

4 to 5 green onions, thinly sliced including some green tops

1/2 cup parsley, chopped (optional)

Grated peel of one orange

2 tablespoons olive oil

Salt to taste

In a medium bowl, combine cherries, apricots and orange juice; microwave one minute to warm juice. Set aside.

Meanwhile, in a heavy medium-size saucepan, combine wild rice and chicken broth and bring to a boil. Reduce heat to a simmer and continue simmering, uncovered, for 45 to 60 minutes, until most of the grains have opened and the rice is tender. Drain and place rice in a mixing bowl.

Drain cherries and apricots but be sure to reserve the juice used for soaking. To the wild rice, add the cherries, apricots, 1/3 cup of the soaking juice (reserve remainder), pecans, green onions, parsley, grated orange peel and olive oil. Toss gently to combine.Taste; add salt as needed.

Allow to stand at least two hours for flavors to blend. Before serving, taste again and adjust seasonings. If needed for moisture, add remaining orange juice. Best served at room temperature.

Serves six to eight

Sylvia Rector, *Detroit Free Press* food writer and restaurant critic

Leelanau Country Inn's Cherry Pungent Fruit Sauce

1 15.5-ounce jar cherry preserves*
1 tablespoon horseradish
1 tablespoon fresh lemon juice
1 teaspoon dry mustard
1 teaspoon ground ginger
1/8 teapoon Tabasco sauce

Combine all ingredients in a blender and blend for 15 to 20 seconds. Serve at room temperature or chilled. May be stored under refrigeration for up to 3 weeks.

* Various preserves or marmalades may be substituted to change the character of the sauce. The sauce also is a fine accompaniment to poultry entrees, grilled shrimp and pork tenderloin. Also use on top of cream cheese as a cracker spread.

Makes one and one half cups

Leelanau Country Inn's Cookery...Continued

Orange-Wild Rice Salad with Smoked Turkey

6 cups water
1 cup uncooked wild rice
1 cup orange sections (about 4
    oranges)
1/2 cup diced celery
1/3 cup dried sweet cherries
1/2 pound smoked turkey breast,
    diced

Dressing:
1/4 cup thawed orange juice
    concentrate, undiluted
2 tablespoons fresh lemon juice
2 tablespoons water
1 tablespoon Dijon mustard
1 1/2 teaspoons olive oil
1/2 teaspoon salt
1/4 teaspoon freshly ground black
    pepper

Salad:
Bring water to a boil in a medium saucepan; stir in rice. Partially cover, reduce heat, and simmer 1 hour or until tender. Drain; cool. Place rice, oranges, celery, cherries and turkey in a bowl.

Dressing:
Combine orange juice concentrate and remaining ingredients; stir well with a whisk. Pour over rice mixture; toss well. Cover and chill.

Cooking Light

Jacquie Caters Broccoli Salad

8 cups broccoli florets, rinsed and
    drained
12 strips bacon, cooked, drained and
    crumbled
$1/2$ cup shelled, salted sunflower seeds
1 cup dried tart cherries
$1^1/2$ cups mayonnaise
4 tablespoons raspberry or cherry
    vinegar
$2/3$ cup granulated sugar

Combine broccoli, bacon, sunflower seeds and cherries in a large bowl.

In a small bowl, combine mayonnaise, vinegar and sugar; mix until smooth. Pour mayonnaise mixture over broccoli mixture; mix until ingredients are well coated.

Refrigerate, covered, until ready to serve.

Serves eight to twelve

Jacquie Honea of Jacquie Caters, Traverse City, Michigan

La Bécasse Salad of Chevre and Dried Cherries

2/3 cup walnut oil or extra virgin olive oil

1/3 cup white wine tarragon vinegar

1 tablespoon tarragon, minced fresh or use1 teaspoon, dried and crumbled

1 teaspoon red bell pepper, finely chopped

1 teaspoon Dijon mustard

1 teaspoon fresh lemon juice

1/2 teaspoon salt

6 to 8 twists of fresh black pepper

1/2 pound spinach

1/2 head romaine lettuce

6 ounces chevre, crumbled (goat cheese)

3/4 cup dried cherries

3/4 cup almonds, toasted and sliced

1/2 red onion, finely sliced

1/2 red bell pepper, diced

Whisk together olive oil, vinegar, tarragon, bell pepper, mustard, lemon juice, salt and pepper. Wash and clean spinach and romaine. Tear into bite-size pieces. Toss with 3/4 cup vinaigrette. Arrange on plates. Sprinkle each plate with chevre, cherries, almonds, red onion and bell pepper.

Drizzle with remaining vinaigrette.

Serves six

La Bécasse, Burdickville, Michigan near Glen Lake

Acorn Squash Bake

2 acorn squash
$1/4$ cup butter, melted
$1/2$ cup dried tart cherries
$1/4$ cup chopped pecans
3 tablespoons firmly packed light brown sugar
$1/2$ teaspoon cinnamon or nutmeg

Preheat oven to 350 degrees.

Cut each acorn squash in half. Remove seeds and fiber. Place cut side down in baking pan with small amount of water in bottom. Bake for 45 to 50 minutes or until squash is tender and can be pierced with a fork. (Or place squash cut side down in a microwave-safe container. Add a little water. Microwave on High (100% power) 5 to 7 minutes, turning dish once. Continue cooking, if necessary, until squash is tender.)

Meanwhile, combine butter, cherries, pecans, brown sugar and cinnamon or nutmeg. Heat on top of stove or in microwave oven until butter melts. Fill center of each squash half with one-quarter of the cherry mixture. Mix some of the cooked squash with the cherry filling. Serve immediately.

serves four

Cherry Marketing Institute

Carrots with Charisma

1 pound carrots, peeled and sliced
$^1/_2$ cup dried tart cherries
3 tablespoons pure maple syrup
2 tablespoons butter
$^1/_2$ teaspoon fresh ground nutmeg
$^1/_4$ teaspoon fresh ground ginger
$^1/_2$ cup walnuts

Cook carrots in water in a covered 2-quart saucepan 8 to 10 minutes, or until tender. Drain well.

Add dried cherries, maple syrup, butter, nutmeg and ginger to cooked carrots; mix to combine ingredients.

Cook, stirring occasionally, over medium heat, 3 to 4 minutes, or until sauce is bubbly.

Toast walnuts in a dry skillet on the stovetop or in a shallow baking pan under the broiler, add to carrot mixture and serve immediately.

serves six

Cherry Marketing Institute

Winter Cherry Salad

1 cup dried tart cherries
2 large naval oranges, peeled and sectioned
2 kiwi fruit, peeled and sliced
$1/4$ cup orange juice
$1/4$ teaspoon fresh ground cinnamon
$1/4$ cup slivered almonds, toasted

Put dried cherries, orange sections and kiwi fruit slices in a salad bowl. Combine orange juice and cinnamon in a small bowl; mix well. Pour orange juice mixture over fruit mixture; mix gently.

Refrigerate, covered, 1 to 2 hours, stirring occasionally. Sprinkle with toasted almonds just before serving.

Serves six

Cherry Marketing Institute

Mike Boudjalis' Cherry Turkey Salad

2 pound pulled turkey, chopped into
$1/2$-inch pieces
1 cup dried cherries
1 cup toasted pecans
1 cup mayonnaise
1 cup fresh celery, chopped into
$1/4$-inch pieces
$1/4$ cup fresh parsley, finely chopped
$1/4$ cup green onion, finely chopped

Combine ingredients and gently fold together.

Top on a bed of fresh chopped greens. Also makes a delicious sandwich.

Mike Boudjalis, Mary's Kitchen Port, Traverse City

Cherry Pink and Apple Blossom White

It's cherry pink and apple blossom white,
When your true lover comes your way.
It's cherry pink and apple blossom white
The poets say.

The story goes that once a cherry tree
Beside an apple tree did grow.
And there a boy once met his bride to be
long, long ago.

It's cherry pink and apple blossom white,
When you're in love.

French words by Jacques Larue
English words by Mack David
Music by Louiguy

Spinach Salad with Cherries

Salad:
5 cups fresh baby spinach, washed
$1/2$ cup dried tart cherries
$1/2$ cup red onion, thinly sliced
feta cheese, crumbled

Dressing:
$1/4$ cup olive oil
$1/4$ cup red wine vinegar
2 teaspoons honey
$1/8$ teaspoon freshly ground black
      pepper

For the salad:
Combine spinach, cherries and onion in a large salad bowl. Spoon dressing over spinach mixture; mix to coat salad with dressing. Serve topped with feta cheese.

For the dressing:
Combine oil, vinegar, honey and pepper in a medium bowl; mix well.

Serves four

Cherry Marketing Institute

82

Cherry and Smoked Turkey Salad

Salad:

12 ounces smoked turkey, diced

1 cup diced tart cherries

1 mango or large nectarine, pared and
     sliced

1 kiwi fruit, sliced

Napa cabbage, shredded

Spicy Dressing:

2 tablespoon extra-virgin olive oil

1 large clove garlic, crushed

2 tablespoons balsamic or red wine
     vinegar

1 tablespoon honey

1 tablespoon hot mustard

2 teaspoons grated fresh ginger

1/2 teaspoon salt

Arrange turkey, cherries, mango and kiwi fruit on shredded Napa cabbage.

Combine ingredients for dressing and mix well. Drizzle dressing over the salad

Serves four

Washington State Fruit Commission

Cherry Marinade for Chicken or Pork

1 cup soy sauce

1/2 cup Worcestershire sauce

1 cup red wine

1/4 cup molasses

1/2 cup chile sauce

1/2 cup balsamic vinegar

1 cup cherry concentrate (see sources)

1 cup salad oil

1 tablespoon garlic, minced

1 cup fresh or frozen cherries, pureed

1/2 teaspoon hot pepper sauce

1 teaspoon pepper

Combine all ingredients in a large bowl. Mix well. Arrange meat in a non-corrosive dish and cover with the marinade. Reserve the remaining marinade for future use. Do not reuse the marinade that has come into contact with raw meat.

Makes five cups

Northwestern Michigan College Culinary Arts Department

Café Bliss' Tart Cherry Maple Chutney

1 cup finely diced red onion
2 teaspoon finely diced garlic
$1/4$ cup olive oil
5 pounds pitted tart cherries
2 cups maple syrup
$1/2$ cup honey
$1/2$ cup red wine vinegar
$1/2$ cup balsamic vinegar
$1/2$ cup corn starch
1 cup water

Saute' the garlic and onion in oil until tender. Add the cherries, syrup, honey and vinegar and bring to temperature (180 degrees), stirring often. In a separate bowl, whisk the corn starch into water until it dissolves and slowly add it to the hot mixture, stirring constantly until thickened (it will thicken to about the same viscosity as maple syrup). Remove from heat.

The chutney can be refrigerated for several weeks or it can be bottled with the inversion canning method (no hot water bath required). Using sterilized jars and lids, fill jar with hot chutney to1/2 inch of the lip, tighten the lid, invert for one minute, rinse jars in hot water, and the product will have a shelf life of 3-5 years.

Ingredients may be halved for a smaller batch.

Makes six-plus pints.

T.J. Johnson, chef/proprietor, Café Bliss, Suttons Bay, Michigan

Cherry BBQ Sauce

1 quart ketchup
12 ounces cherry preserves
8 strips bacon, diced
1 yellow onion, diced
$^1/_4$ cup Worcestershire
1 tablespoon dry mustard
$^1/_4$ cup red wine vinegar

In a heavy skillet, render the fat from bacon. Remove pieces and reserve. Add onion to the fat and saute' until opaque. Add remaining ingredients and bring to a boil. Reduce heat and simmer on low heat for 15 to 20 minutes. BBQ sauce will keep for several weeks in the refrigerator.

Makes two quarts

Northwestern Michigan College Culinary Arts Department

Cherry Vinaigrette Style Dressing

1 pint cherries, tart, frozen, puréed
1/2 ounce arrowroot
4 fluid ounces honey
8 fluid ounces red wine vinegar
12 fluid ounces extra virgin olive oil
2 fluid ounces cherry juice concentrate
1/2 teaspoon fresh ground clove
1 teaspoon freshly ground black
    pepper
1/2 teaspoon salt

Dissolve the arrowroot in a small amount of puréed cherries.

Bring the puréed cherries to a boil. Add the honey. Gradually add the arrowroot to the hot purée. Cook until it is thin enough to coat the back of a spoon. Cool puréed cherry mixture to room temperature.

Whip in vinegar and oil. Add cherry juice concentrate and seasonings.

Makes one quart

Northwestern Michigan College Culinary Arts Department

Forteen-thousand Montmorency cherry trees planted in 1912 formed Cherry Home, the world's largest red tart cherry orchard at that time. Located at the northern most tip of Michigan's Leelanau County, Cherry Home employed cherry pickers and sorters whose pay depended on picking speed. In 1932, a picker would earn 10 cents a lug, and sorters, 15 cents an hour with 5 cents deducted for lunch.

Thai Beef Cherry Salad

1 pound beef, top round, fat trimmed,
    cut into 2-inch strips
$1/3$ cup chili peppers
juice of 1 lime
juice of 1 lemon
1 cup oyster sauce
$1/2$ cup red onion, thinly sliced
1 cup cucumbers, peeled, cut in half
    lengthwise, sliced 1/4 inch
4 cloves garlic, minced
1 cup dried cherries, coarsely
    chopped
$1/2$ cup green onions, sliced
3 cups green cabbage, shredded
1 teaspoon black pepper

Saute' beef with the garlic chilies.

Combine lime and lemon juice and oyster sauce. Add remaining ingredients and toss to coat evenly.

If desired, serve on rice.

Serves four

Northwestern Michigan College Culinary Arts Department

Gail's Green Salad with Cherries

Salad:

6 cups lettuce leaves, washed and
    dried
4 ounces blue cheese, crumbled
1 apple, cored and sliced $1/4$ inch
$1/2$ cup red onion, thinly sliced
1 cup walnuts, toasted
$1/2$ cup dried cherries

Dressing:

$1/4$ cup red wine vinegar
2 tablespoons vegetable oil
2 tablespoons sugar
$1/2$ teaspoons salt
dash ground black pepper
$1/4$ teaspoon rosemary, crushed
$1/4$ teaspoon thyme

Arrange lettuce, blue cheese, red onion, walnuts, and dried cherries in a large salad bowl; set aside.

In a small bowl, mix together the dressing ingredients until well combined and sugar and salt are dissolved.

Serve lettuce with dressing on the side for individual tastes.

Serves six

Gail Lange, The Cherry Stop, downtown Traverse City, Michigan

Cherry Grilled Sweet Pepper Salad

1/4 cup balsamic vinegar
2 tablespoons olive oil
1 clove garlic, minced
2 tablespoons basil leaves, finely
    chopped
1 teaspoon salt
1/4 teaspoon freshly ground
    black pepper
2 cups fresh or frozen sweet cherries
1 cup sweet onion, thinly sliced
2 yellow bell peppers, washed, halved
    and seeded
2 red bell peppers, washed, halved
    and seeded

In a large bowl, combine the balsamic vinegar, olive oil, garlic, basil, salt and pepper; mix well. Remove about 2 tablespoons of the dressing to a separate small bowl for the peppers. Toss the cherries and onions in the remaining dressing; set aside.

Prepare the bell pepper halves with some of the reserved dressing. Grill over medium heat on a lightly oiled grill for 10 to 12 minutes. Turn and brush the peppers with dressing halfway through the grilling. Alternatively, place the peppers on a broiler rack and broil the peppers until the skins are slightly charred, then turn over, brush with dressing and continue cooking.

Place the peppers in a paper or plastic food bag and close tightly; let stand 10 to 15 minutes. Remove from the bag, peel off and discard the skin. Slice the peppers into 1/2- inch strips and mix with the cherry mixture.

Serve with grilled meats or use on sandwiches in place of relishes.

Serves six

Northwest Cherry Growers, Yakima, Washington

Mainstays

Sweet and Sour Beef Stew with Dried Cherries

3 tablespoons all-purpose flour

1 $1/4$ teaspoons salt

$1/2$ teaspoon ground allspice

$1/2$ teaspoon ground cinnamon

$1/2$ teaspoon pepper

2 pounds boneless beef chuck, cut into
    1-inch cubes

4 tablespoons vegetable oil

2 large onions, thinly sliced

1 cup dried cherries

2 tablespoons sugar

2 tablespoons red wine vinegar

2 tablespoons water

1 cup dry red wine

1 cup beef stock or canned broth

$1/2$-pound button mushrooms,
    trimmed and quartered

Preheat oven to 350 degrees with rack in center position.

Combine flour, salt, allspice, cinnamon, and pepper in a large plastic bag. Add beef to bag and toss, coating pieces evenly with seasoned flour.

Heat one tablespoon oil in heavy skillet over medium-high heat. Add one-third of beef and cook until brown, about 5 minutes. Transfer meat to a Dutch oven, using a slotted spoon. Repeat with remaining meat in two batches, adding 1 tablespoon oil to skillet each time. Add remaining oil to same skillet. Stirring frequently, add onions and cherries and cook until onions are soft and light brown, about 12 minutes. Mix in sugar, vinegar, and water. Increase heat to high and cook until brown, stirring frequently, about 8 minutes. Add onion mixture to beef in Dutch oven. Mix in wine, stock, and mushrooms; cover tightly and bake until beef is tender, about 2 hours 15 minutes, uncovering stew during the last 2 minutes if liquid is too thin. Serve or cover and refrigerate. Stew can be prepared 2 days ahead. Bring to room temperature first and reheat over low.

Serves six

The Culinary Collection - recipe by Michelle Morouse

Beef and Cherry Satay

1¹/2-pounds beef, round, fat trimmed
2 tablespoons sesame oil
¹/4 cup soy sauce
¹/2 teaspoon garlic powder
1 tablespoon apple cider vinegar
¹/2 teaspoon black pepper
¹/2 teaspoon cayenne pepper
³/4 cup cherry juice concentrate
1 tablespoon dried onions
¹/2 cup peanut sauce

Peanut Sauce:
2 cups chicken stock
¹/2 cup cherry juice concentrate
1 cup peanut butter

For Beef:
Cut beef into thin strips. Mix remaining ingredients and marinate meat for at least 24 hours. Remove meat and grill. Serve with peanut sauce

For Peanut Sauce:
Mix chicken stock and cherry juice together and heat. Simmer mixture for 15 to 20 minutes and then add peanut butter. Stir to desired consistency.

Serves sixteen

Northwestern Michigan College Culinary ArtsDepartment

Beef Burgundy

2^1/2 pounds sirloin steak
4 cloves garlic, chopped
^{1}/2 cup chopped onion
2 cups dry red wine
1 10-ounce can reduced fat condensed
    cream of mushroom soup,
    undiluted
1^1/2 cups dried tart cherries
^{1}/2 pound fresh mushrooms, cleaned
    and sliced
3 tablespoons all-purpose flour
^{1}/2 cup water
egg noodles or bow-tie pasta, cooked
    and well drained

Preheat oven to 350 degrees.

Trim fat from sirloin and cut steak into 1-inch cubes. Coat a large, oven-proof Dutch oven or stockpot with non-stick cooking spray.

Place over medium heat until hot. Add steak, cook, stirring occasionally, 8 to 10 minutes, or until meat is brown. Drain well and set aside.

Recoat pan with cooking spray, place over medium heat. Add garlic and onion; saute' for 1 minute. Add wine, mushroom soup and mushrooms; mix well. Bring mixture to a boil. Return steak to pan, stir in cherries.

Combine flour and water in a small bowl; blended until smooth with a fork or wire wisk. Gradually stir flour mixture into steak mixture; mix well. Bake covered for 1^1/2 hours, or until steak is tender and mixture is thick. Serve over cooked noodles or pasta.

Serves eight

Chicken and Wild Mushroom Strudel
with Dried Cherries

3/4 cup butter, divided
4 tablespoons flour
2 cups chicken stock
1/2 cup heavy cream
1 tablespoon rosemary, fresh, crushed
2 tablespoons dry white wine
3 cups chicken, diced, cooked
1 1/2 cups diced wild mushrooms
1 cup dried cherries
phyllo dough, thawed
sour cream (optional)
rosemary for garnish

Preheat oven to 350 degrees.

Combine 4 tablespoons butter and flour in a saucepan. Cook over low heat for at least 5 minutes. Slowly add stock, cream, rosemary and white wine. Simmer for at least 10 minutes. Add chicken, mushrooms and cherries.

Melt remaining butter. Using pastry brush, butter 6 sheets of phyllo dough, layering one on top of the other. Place a layer (2 inches wide by 1 inch thick) of chicken mixture on phyllo dough. Fold dough from left side over filling. Roll remaining dough around filling, brushing lightly with butter to seal as needed. Repeat with remaining phyllo and chicken mixture.

Bake for 15 to 20 minutes or until golden on top. Serve immediately with a dollop of sour cream and a sprig of rosemary.

Serves eight

Adapted from *Bountiful Arbor*

Chicken Breasts in Phyllo

1 1/2 cups mayonnaise

1 cup chopped scallions

1/3 cup lemon juice

2 cloves garlic, minced

2 teaspoons dried tarragon

1/4 cup dried cherries

12 boneless chicken breasts halves

salt and pepper

20 tablespoons (2 1/2 sticks) butter, melted

24 sheets phyllo dough (about 1 pound)

1/3 cup freshly grated parmesan cheese

Preheat oven to 375 degrees.

Combine the mayonnaise, scallions, lemon juice, garlic, tarragon and cherries to make a sauce. Lightly sprinkle the chicken pieces with salt and pepper. Unroll the phyllo; cover with waxed paper and then with a damp kitchen towel to keep it from drying out. Place a sheet of phyllo on a flat surface. Brush with melted butter (about 2 teaspoons). Place a second sheet on top of the first. Brush with melted butter. Spread about 1 1/2 tablespoons of sauce on each side of chicken breast (3 tablespoons in all). Place the breast on one end of the buttered phyllo sheets. Fold the corner over the breast, then fold the sides over and roll the breast up to form a package. Place in an ungreased baking dish. Repeat with the remaining breasts and phyllo sheets, keeping the unused phyllo covered until ready to use. Brush the packets with the rest of the melted butter and sprinkle with Parmesan cheese. The dish may be tightly sealed and frozen. Thaw completely before baking. Bake for 25 to 35 minutes, or until golden brown. Serve hot.

Serves twelve

Adapted from *Junior League Centennial Cookbook*

Cornish Game Hens Stuffed with Couscous

4 cornish game hens
1 pound couscous
2 tablespoons vegetable oil (for the almonds)
$^1/_2$ pound blanched almonds
$^1/_2$ pound dried cherries
2 tablespoons confectioners sugar
1 tablespoon ground cinnamon
1 teaspoon ground ginger
1 pinch powdered saffron
4 tablespoons butter, softened
4 garlic cloves, peeled and crushed
$^1/_2$ teaspoon salt
freshly ground pepper
$^1/_2$ teaspoon ground cumin
1 teaspoon paprika

Preheat oven to 375 degrees.

Prepare couscous according to package directions and transfer to large mixing bowl.

Meanwhile, gently fry the almonds in a little oil until golden, then crush or chop them coarsely. Place the cherries in small bowl and cover them with boiling water. Soak for 10 minutes, then drain. Add the almonds, cherries, confectioners sugar, cinnamon, ginger and saffron to the couscous and mix well. Stuff the game hens with the couscous and sew them up (or cover the opening with a piece of foil).

In a separate bowl, mix butter, garlic, salt, pepper, cumin, and paprika to make a paste. Rub the paste all over the game hens. Place them in an ovenproof dish, adding a little water at the bottom of the dish so the butter does not burn. Roast the game hens for about 45 minutes, basting occasionally with the cooking juices. Heat extra stuffing in the oven in a dish covered with foil.

Serves four

Recipes from Morocco

Chicken Cherry Wraps

1/4 cup light sour cream
1/4 cup mayonnaise
1 tablespoon Dijon mustard
1 teaspoon Worcestershire sauce
3/4 teaspoon curry
1/4 teapoon salt
1/4 teaspoon pepper
1 1/2 cup chicken, cooked and finely
    chopped
1 cup dried cherries
1/3 cup shredded carrot
1/4 cup green onion, sliced
4 whole wheat flour tortillas or lavash

Stir together sour cream, mustard, mayonnaise, Worcestershire sauce, curry, salt and pepper in a medium bowl. Gently stir in chicken, carrot, and green onion. Mound about 1/2 to 3/4 cup of the chicken mixture just below the center of the tortilla or lavash. Fold in sides, just covering edges of the chicken mixture. Roll up from one side to form a wrap.

*Add sunflower seeds for extra crunch

Serves four

Cherry Point Chicken Stroganoff

3/4 cup cherry wine, divided
Thyme, sage, ground ginger and
    rosemary
6 boneless, skinless chicken breast
    halves
2 tablespoons olive oil
1 tablespoon garlic, minced
1/2 pound fresh mushrooms, cleaned
    and sliced
1/3 cup walnuts, coarsely chopped
1/3 cup dried cherries
8 ounces (1 cup) sour cream
salt and pepper to taste
1 tablespoon butter
1 pound curly egg noodles, cooked
    fresh parsley, carrot curls and
    cherry tomatoes for garnish

For marinade:
In a large, nonreactive bowl, mix 1/4 cup of the cherry wine, a pinch each of thyme, sage and ginger. Add the chicken breasts, and marinate, covered, for one hour in refrigerator.

In a large nonreactive frying pan, heat the olive oil over medium heat and add the garlic, searing until lightly browned. Add a pinch each of sage and ginger and two pinches of rosemary, the chicken breasts and the marinade, and cook down the liquid slightly to caramelize. Turn the breasts after 5-8 minutes. If needed while cooking, add a little more olive oil. Cook another 5-8 minutes. Cook the egg noodles according to package directions. Add another 1/2 cup of the wine, the mushrooms, the chopped walnuts and the dried cherries and cook down the liquid slightly. Remove from the heat, let stand a couple of minutes, fold in the sour cream, season with salt and pepper. Drain the egg noodles well, sprinkle with a bit of olive oil, coarse ground pepper and top with a pat of butter. Then top with the stroganoff and garnish with fresh parsley, carrot curls and cherry tomatoes.

Serves six

Conrad Heiderer, executive chef, Cherry Point Garden Grill, Shelby, MI

Turkey Saute' with Fresh Cherry Sauce

1 tablespoon butter
4 turkey breast cutlets (about $1/2$
    pound)
$1/4$ cup chopped shallots
1 teaspoon dried thyme
$1/4$ cup balsamic vinegar
2 tablespoons water
1 cup fresh sweet cherries, halved,
    pitted
2 tablespoons all-fruit cherry spread

Melt butter in heavy medium skillet over medium-high heat. Sprinkle turkey with salt and pepper. Add turkey to skillet and saute' until golden, about 2 minutes per side. Using tongs, transfer turkey to a plate. Add shallots and thyme to skillet. Reduce heat to medium-low heat and cook 2 minutes, stirring occasionally. Add vinegar and water and bring to a simmer, scraping up any browned bits. Add cherries and fruit spread. Simmer until cherries soften and sauce thickens slightly, stirring occasionally, about 3 minutes. Season sauce to taste with salt and pepper. Return turkey and any collected juices to skillet. Simmer just until cooked through and hot, about 1 minute. Transfer turkey and sauce to plates.

Serves two

Bon Appétit June 1996

People are queer, there're always crowing, scrambling and rushing about;
Why don't they stop someday, address themselves this way?
Why are we here?
Where are we going?
It's time that we found out. We're not here to stay; we're on a short holiday.
Life is just a bowl of cherries.
Don't take it serious; it's too mysterious.
You work, you save, you worry so,
But you can't take your dough when you go, go, go.

—*Life is Just a Bowl of Cherries*
Lyrics by Lew Brown, music by Ray Henderson, 1931

Craig Common's Pork Tenderloin
with Dried Cherry Compote

6 six-ounce pieces of pork tenderloin
6 sprigs fresh rosemary, for garnish

Mustard marinade:
1 cup olive oil
2 cloves garlic
1/3 cup Dijon mustard
2 teaspoons black pepper
1 teaspoon Kosher salt
2 teaspoons thyme, finely chopped
1 teaspoon rosemary, finely chopped

Dried cherry compote:
1/2 small red onion, diced
1/4 cup shiitake mushrooms
1 tablespoon olive oil
3 cups beef stock
1 teaspoon orange zest
2 cups dry red wine
1 cup dried cherries
1/4 cup orange juice
1 tablespoon thyme, chopped
1/2 cup port wine
3 tablespoons butter, chilled, cut into
    pieces

Mustard marinade:
In a blender, puree olive oil and garlic. Add remaining marinade ingredients and blend well. Marinate pork tenderloin in refrigerator for 4 hours or overnight.

Grill or broil tenderloin until medium, approximately 8 to 10 minutes. Slice on bias into 1/4-inch pieces. Ladle cherry compote on serving plate and place pork on top of compote. Garnish with rosemary sprigs.

Dried cherry compote:
Saute' red onions and shiitake mushrooms in olive oil until lightly browned, about 3 to 5 minutes. Add beef stock, orange zest, red wine; bring to a boil and continue cooking until liquid is reduced by half. Add dried cherries, orange juice, thyme and port wine. Return to boil and continue cooking until liquid is of a syrupy consistency. Remove from heat and whisk in chilled butter, one piece at a time. Return to a boil prior to serving.

Serves six

Common Grill, Chelsea, Michigan

Jimmy Schmidt's Grilled Pork Chops and Dried Cherries

1 cup beef or veal stock
1 cup balsamic vinegar
1 cup dried tart cherries
1/2 cup pearl onions, roasted
4 tablespoons (1/2 stick) unsalted
    butter
salt to taste
black pepper, freshly ground, to taste
4 pork loin chops, about 10 ounces
    each, completely trimmed
2 tablespoons extra virgin olive oil
1/4 cup packed fresh sage leaves, finely
    julienned
4 sprigs fresh sage for garnish

Preheat the grill or broiler.

In a large saucepan, combine the stock and vinegar. Bring to a simmer over medium heat and cook until reduced to 1 cup, about 6 minutes.

Add cherries and continue to simmer until thickened enough to coat the back of a spoon, about 4 minutes. Add pearl onions, then whisk in the butter. Adjust the salt and pepper. Reduce the heat to low.

Rub the chops with the olive oil. Place them on the grill or under the broiler and cook until well seared, about 5 minutes. Turn over and cook to desired temperature or medium, about 10 minutes, depending upon the thickness of the chop.

Spoon the sauce onto warm serving plates, reserving 1/4 cup.

Sprinkle the sage across the sauce and position the chops on it. Spoon the remaining sauce over the chops, garnish with herb sprigs, and serve.

Serves four

Honey-Roasted Ham or Turkey with Dried Cherry Relish

1/2 cup crème de cassis (black currant-flavored liqueur) or cherry-flavored brandy

1/2 cup water

1/2 cup sugar

2 cups dried tart cherries or dried Bing cherries or 1 cup of each (about 10 ounces total)

3/4 cup pecans, toasted, chopped (about 3 ounces)

2 tablespoons grated orange peel

1 6-to-8 pound spiral-cut honey-roasted ham or one 12 to14 pound honey-roasted turkey

small dinner rolls, optional

Stir crème de cassis, 1/2 cup water and sugar in heavy medium saucepan over medium heat until sugar dissolves. Bring to boil. Add dried cherries. Reduce heat; cover and simmer until cherries are plump, about 5 minutes. Mix in pecans and orange peel. Season relish lightly with salt. Transfer to bowl. Cool. (Can be made 1 week ahead. Cover and refrigerate.) Place ham or turkey on platter. Place bowl with cherry relish alongside. Serve with dinner rolls, if desired.

Bon Appétit December 1998

Serves twelve to fourteen

Michigan Crown Roast of Pork with Wild Rice Stuffing

wild rice stuffing:
1 cup wild rice
1 teaspoon salt
$1/4$ teaspoon dried thyme
1 bay leaf
2 sprigs parsley, chopped
4 tablespoons ($1/2$ stick) butter
$1/2$ cup mushrooms, sauteed
1 small onion, chopped
2 ribs of celery, chopped
$1/4$ cup pine nuts or pecans (optional)
$1/4$ cup dried cherries

roast of pork:
1 crown roast of pork, 6 to 7 pounds
     (2 ribs per person), backbone
     removed and rib ends
     frenched
Salt, pepper and garlic salt, to
     taste
whole spiced crabapples, 1 for each
     rib

To prepare the stuffing, place the wild rice in a saucepan, cover with cold water, and bring to a boil. Remove from the heat and skim. Drain in a colander. Return to the saucepan and add 3 cups of water, the salt, thyme, bay leaf and chopped parsley. Bring to a boil, reduce the heat to a simmer, cover, and cook about 30 minutes, or until tender. Remove from the heat and drain. Add the butter and blend. Add the sauteed mushrooms, onion, celery, nuts and dried cherries.

Preheat the oven to 325 degrees. Place the roast with the rib ends up on a rack in a shallow pan. Cover each rib end with foil so the bones will not char; season with salt and pepper, and garlic salt. Roast about 30 minutes per pound, or until meat thermometer registers 185 degrees. Halfway through the roasting time, fill the cavity with wild rice stuffing. When the roast is done, place it on a heated platter. Remove the foil from the tips of the ribs and place a spiced crabapple on the end of each rib. To serve, slice downward between the ribs and remove the chops one at a time. Serve each person 2 chops and a spoonful of stuffing

Serves six to eight

Junior League Centennial Cookbook

Keil Moshier's Cherry and Apple Marinade for Pork Tenderloin

1 cup canned cherries in juice (not heavy syrup)
$1/2$ cup frozen sliced apples, thawed and processed
2 tablespoons garlic, minced
2 tablespoons honey
$1/2$ cup red wine vinegar
1 tablespoon salt
2 teaspoons cracked black pepper
$1/2$ cup diced yellow onion
2 cups vegetable oil
6 to 8 whole pork tenderloins

For Apple-Cherry Relish:
2 medium fresh apples, diced
1 cup tart pitted cherries, rinsed thoroughly
$1/4$ cup red onion
2 tablespoons apple cider vinegar
2 teaspoons minced garlic
1 tablespoon light corn syrup
Pinch salt
Pinch black pepper, cracked
2 tablespoons parsley, chopped

Combine ingredients in a bowl and mix together. Process in a food processor until smooth and everything is incorporated. If you do not have a food processor, a mixer or hand held blender works also.

Clean the silver skin off the tenderloins and cut them halfway through, the full length of the loin. Drop into the marinade in a nonreactive dish; cover and marinate overnight in the refrigerator.

Remove the loins from the marinade and scrape off the excess marinade, as it will flare up on the grill. Grill the pork over a HOT fire to 160 degrees, about 7 to 8 minutes on each side. Remove from fire, allow to rest for a few minutes, then slice into medallions and top with apple cherry relish or fall fruit chutney (recipes below).

For Apple-Cherry Relish:
Dice apples, cherries, celery and onion to a $1/4$-inch in size and combine with other ingredients. Allow to set overnight in the cooler before using.

Serves ten to twelve

Keil Moshier, Executive Chef , Bowers Harbor Inn,, Traverse City, MI.

Pork Loin with Cherry Almond Sauce

1 boned and tied pork loin roast, 4 to
    6 pounds
1 (12- ounce) jar cherry preserves
$1/4$ cup light corn syrup
$1/4$ cup red wine vinegar
$1/4$ teaspoon salt
$1/4$ teaspoon grated nutmeg
$1/4$ teaspoon ground cloves
$1/4$ teaspoon ground cinnamon
$1/8$ teaspoon ground black pepper
$1/4$ cup slivered blanched almonds

Preheat oven to 325 degrees.

Put pork on a rack in a shallow roasting pan. Place in the oven and roast uncovered about 3 hours.

Meanwhile, combine the cherry preserves, corn syrup, vinegar, salt, and spices. Bring to a boil and boil for 1 minute. Add the almonds. Baste the meat with the sauce several times during the last 30 minutes of roasting time.

Serve the remaining sauce with the meat.

Serves eight

Junior League Centennial Cookbook

109

Brined Pork Loin
with Onion, Cherry and Garlic Compote

8 cups water

$1/2$ cup coarse salt

$1/2$ cup packed brown sugar

1 tablespoon fennel seeds

1 tablespoon coriander seeds

1 tablespoon whole black peppercorns

3 bay leaves

1 center-cut boneless pork loin roast
(about 4 pounds)

1 tablespoon olive oil

2 teaspoons chopped fresh sage

2 teaspoons chopped fresh rosemary

2 teaspoons chopped fresh thyme

2 teaspoons chopped fresh marjoram

Onion, Cherry, and Garlic Compote
(see next page)

Combine first 7 ingredients in heavy large pot. Bring to simmer over medium heat , stirring to dissolve salt and sugar. Remove from heat. Cool to room temperature. Transfer brine to a very large bowl. Add pork (weight pork with a plate to keep below surface.) Cover; refrigerate overnight. Drain pork. Return pork to bowl, cover with water (weight pork with plate). Soak at room temperature 2 hours.

Position rack in top third of oven and preheat to 350 degrees. Drain pork. Pat dry. Transfer to rack set in large roasting pan. Rub pork all over with oil. Sprinkle with fresh herbs, pressing to adhere. Sprinkle with pepper. Roast until thermometer inserted into center of pork registers 150 degrees, about 1 hour 40 minutes. Transfer pork to cutting board; tent with foil. Let stand 10 minutes. Cut pork into $1/4$ to $1/2$ inch-thick slices.

Serve with compote.

Serves eight

Bon Appetit

Onion, Cherry and Garlic Compote

1 pound pearl onions
$^1/_4$ cup butter, ($^1/_2$ stick)
24 garlic cloves, peeled
1 bay leaf
$1^1/_2$ cups tawny Port
$^1/_4$ cup white wine vinegar
4 teaspoons sugar
$^1/_2$ teaspoon salt
$^1/_2$ cup dried cherries
$1^1/_2$ teaspoons chopped thyme

Bring large saucepan of water to a boil. Add onions. Boil 2 minutes. Drain. Rinse under cold water. Peel onion. Trim root end slightly, leaving root base intact.

Melt butter in heavy medium saucepan over medium-low heat. Add garlic and bay leaf. Saute' until garlic is golden brown, about 6 minutes. Add Port, vinegar, sugar and salt. Simmer 8 minutes. Add onions and cherries. Simmer until onions are tender, stirring occasionally, about 9 minutes. Remove from heat. Stir in thyme. Discard bay leaf. Season with salt and pepper.

(Can be made 1 day ahead. Cover and refrigerate. Rewarm over medium heat before serving.) Serve warm.

Makes two cups

Adapted from *Bon Appetit March 2002*

Patty's Zippy Pork Tenderloin

1 1/2 to 2-pound pork tenderloin
1 1/2 cups orange juice
zest from 1 orange
1/4 cup dried tart **cherries**, chopped
1 large jalapeno pepper, seeded and
      chopped medium
2 tablespoons extra virgin olive oil
2 to 3 tablespoons heavy cream

Butterfly the tenderloin and set aside. In a small mixing bowl combine the orange juice, zest, tart cherries, jalapeno and olive oil. Mix well and pour into a gallon size reclosable plastic bag or nonreactive dish. Add the tenderloin and cover. Refrigerate for two to four hours, turning occasionally.

Preheat the broiler on high. Remove the tenderloin from the marinade and place the meat on a lightly oiled broiler pan. Broil 6 to 8 minutes on each side.

Meanwhile, pour the marinade into a small saucepan and heat to a boil, reducing the liquid by half. Reduce heat to a simmer and add the heavy cream, stirring constantly until a smooth consistency is achieved, about two minutes. The sauce will be a medium thickness, but will impart a magnificently tangy-hot flavor.

Remove tenderloin from rack. Cut into 1/4-inch slices on the diagonal. Pour sauce over the slices and serve immediately.

Serves two to four

Patty LaNoue Stearns

Cherry Beer-Marinated Pork Tenderloin

3 pork tenderloins 14 to 16
    ounces each
$1/2$ cup soy sauce
12 ounces **cherry** beer, (Sam Adams
    Cherry Wheat)
$1/3$ cup brown sugar, firmly packed
1 $1/2$ tablespoons fresh ginger, grated
1 teaspoon black pepper
2 tablespoons garlic, minced

Clean fat and silver skin from pork. Combine the marinade ingredients, stirring until the sugar dissolves.

Place tenderloins in a non-corrosive pan and pour the marinade over the top. Cover and let marinate for 2 to 6 hours. Remove from the marinade and grill over medium heat until internal temperature is 150 degrees.

Allow cooked tenderloin to rest for several minutes before cutting.

Serves six

Northwestern Michigan College Culinary Arts Department

Cherry Pork Stir-Fry

1 cup converted rice
1 1/2 pounds pork butt
1/2 cup Spanish onions, halved and
    cut into 1/4-inch strips
1/2 cup green peppers, halved and cut
    into 1/4-inch strips
1/2 cup carrots, sliced julienned
1/2 cup celery, sliced on the bias,
    1/4-inch
1/4 cup water chestnuts
1/4 cup dried cherries
1 tablespoon sesame oil
1 1/2 tablespoons cornstarch
4 cups chicken stock
2 tablespoons cherry juice
    concentrate
1/4 cup soy sauce

Prepare rice according to package directions. Cut pork butt into 2 inch by 1/2-inch strips.

Stir fry.

For liquid use chicken stock mixed with cherry juice concentrate, soy sauce and cornstarch.

Serve over rice

Serves twelve

Northwestern Michigan College Culinary Arts

Leelanau Country Inn's Grilled Shrimp

20 jumbo-jumbo shrimp*
5 cups cherry vinaigrette dressing (see
　　　recipe page in index)
8 skewers
$1/2$ cup cherry pungent fruit sauce (see
　　　page 73)
2 tablespoons fresh parsley, chopped

Note: U-10 shrimp, (signifying 10 shrimp per pound) work best for grilling. Also, look for shrimp labeled "E-Z peel shrimp." They have been cleaned and the shell pulls off easily. Do not use cooked shrimp.

Remove shrimp from the shell and butterfly the shrimp by carefully inserting sharp knife into the large end of the shrimp cutting in about $3/4$ of the way to the back, then cutting to the tail. Be careful not to cut through the shrimp. Rinse and set aside. Dividing shrimp into 4 portions of 5 shrimp, using 2 skewers, pierce the head end of the shrimp with 1 skewer and the midsection with the others, stabilizing it during grilling.

Cooking over an open flame chargrill, preheated so that the rack is HOT. This will sear the shrimp, preventing it from sticking to the rack.

Pour 4 $1/2$ cups cherry vinaigrette in a pan large enough to lay the 4 double skewers flat and marinate refrigerated for 1 hour. In a large saute' pan, heat the remaining cherry vinaigrette so that it is HOT.

Chargrill each double skewer for 2 minutes on each side. Remove the shrimp from skewers and saute' in the hot vinaigrette for 5 minutes or until fully cooked. Be sure to turn shrimp frequently so that all areas cook evenly. Serve with Cherry Pungent Fruit Sauce and top with chopped parsley.

Serves four

Leelanau Country Inn Cookery...Continued

Nancy Allen's Cherry Balm Sauce over Grilled Lamb Chops

8 lamb chops, cut at least $1^1/4$ inches
    thick
extra virgin olive oil
$1/2$ cup dried tart **cherries**
$1^1/2$ cups balsamic vinegar
1 ounce or 2 tablespoons unsalted
    butter, more to taste
2 teaspoons maple syrup
Kosher salt
2 tablespoons finely sliced basil leaves
    or chopped flat leaf parsley
    leaves

Prepare your grill.

Remove the chops from the refrigerator and coat them liberally with olive oil. Set them aside until the grill is ready. While the grill heats, combine the dried cherries and balsamic vinegar in a nonreactive (not aluminum) nine-inch skillet or saucepan. Bring them to a boil over high heat.

Lower the heat to medium. We want the mixture to bubble merrily, not boil furiously. Slow boil the sauce until it begins to be syrupy, about 8 minutes. Whisk in the butter and maple syrup and continue to merrily boil the sauce for another minute or until it thickens a bit more—enough to nicely coat the back of a spoon. Beware, if you go too far you'll end up with tar. Season with salt (and freshly ground pepper if you like).

Sprinkle the chops with salt and set them on the grill. Cook chops until medium-rare. Timing depends on the temperature of your grill and the thickness of your chop—with a kettle grill (top on and vents open) and charcoal, these chops will take 3 to 5 minutes per side. Press the meat with your finger to determine how cooked it is—if it is very soft, it's still rare; if it is springy but still a bit soft—it's medium rare; if your finger meets resistance, the meat is well done.

Pull the meat BEFORE it is done. The heat from the outside of the meat will carry over and finish cooking the inside—raising the internal temperature around 5 degrees. You may purchase a digital instant-read thermometer and take the meat's temperature. Rare is 120 to 130 degrees F; medium rare is 130 to 140 degrees F; medium is 140 to 150 degrees F; and well done is 165 degrees F to 185 degrees F (at which point you could use the chop for a golf ball).

Arrange two lamb chops on each plate and spoon a tablespoon or two of the sauce over them. Garnish with basil or flat leaf parsley.

You may serve this with polenta, potatoes or on pasta. Cherry balm sauce is sensational with grilled duck breast too.

Serves four

Ali Barker's Crab Cakes
with Michigan Sour Cherry Salsa

Crabcakes:
1 1/2 pounds good quality crabmeat (preferably Maryland lump)
3/4 pound bread crumbs, freshly ground
1 teaspoon Worcestershire sauce
1 tablespoon horseradish, freshly grated
1 teaspoon cayenne pepper
2 teaspoons kosher salt
3/4 cup mayonnaise

Salsa:
1 pound fresh sour cherries, pitted
1 large sweet onion
1/2 cup sugar
1/3 cup champagne vinegar
1 teaspoon ground cumin
1/3 cup dried currants
1 tablespoon cracked coriander seed
salt and pepper to taste

Assemble the crab cakes:
Preheat broiler.
Stir together all ingredients except crabmeat; mix well. Add the crab and very gently incorporate into the mix. Try and keep as many large chunks of crabmeat as possible. Chill for 30 minutes.

Prepare the salsa:
Preheat a grill over medium heat, or preheat oven to 400 degrees. Peel and slice the onion into 1/4-inch thick slices. Grill both sides until marked and tender, about 6 minutes a side. Allow to cool, then chop into 1/4-inch pieces.

Bring the sugar, vinegar, and cumin to a simmer in a 1-quart saucepan over high heat, until sugar dissolves and begins to caramelize. Add the onions, currants and coriander seed and cook at a low simmer for 3 minutes. Add cherries and heat through. Adjust the seasoning with salt and pepper to taste.

Finish crab cakes:
Form the chilled crab cakes into 12 two-ounce cakes and place on a cookie sheet. Broil each side for about 3 minutes, or until golden brown. Serve with generous portion of salsa over the top.

Serves four

Ali Barker, executive chef, Bistro on the Boulevard, St. Joseph, Michigan

Cherry Kabobs

2 cups frozen sweet cherries
2 cups pineapple chunks
$1/2$ cup red wine vinegar
2 tablespoons olive oil
1 tablespoon honey
$1/2$ teaspoon curry powder

Partly thaw cherries, then thread them alternately with pineapple chunks on bamboo skewers. Combine vinegar, oil, honey and curry powder in a small bowl; mix well. Place kabobs on broiler pan; broil 4 to 6 inches from heat. (Or grill over medium coals.) Brush with curry mixture. Cook 4 to 5 minutes, turning and basting with additional sauce after each turn.

Serves six

Cherry Marketing Institute

Sweet Things

Old-Fashioned Cherry Vanilla Pie

For dough:
1^1/2 sticks (^{3}/4 cup) cold unsalted
        butter
2^1/2 cups all-purpose flour
^{1}/2 teaspoon salt
^{1}/4 cup cold vegetable shortening
5 to 7 tablespoons ice water

For cherry filling:
1 cup plus 2 tablespoons sugar
^{1}/4 cup quick-cooking tapioca
^{1}/2 teaspoon salt
^{1}/2 teaspoon cinnamon
6 cups fresh or frozen pitted tart
        cherries (about 3 ^{1}/2 pints fresh,
        picked over)
2 tablespoons vanilla
1 tablespoon sugar

Accompaniment: vanilla ice cream

Make dough:
Cut butter into pieces. In a bowl with a pastry blender or in a food processor blend or pulse together flour, salt, butter and shortening until mixture resembles coarse meal. Add 5 tablespoons ice water and toss or pulse just until mixture forms a dough, adding additional ice water, a little at a time, if dough is too dry. Divide dough in half and flatten each piece into a disk. Chill dough, wrapped in plastic wrap, at least 30 minutes and up to 3 days.

Make filling:
In a small bowl stir together sugar, tapioca, salt and cinnamon. In a large heavy skillet cook fresh or frozen cherries over moderately high heat, stirring, until slightly softened, about 2 minutes. With a slotted spoon transfer cherries to a heatproof bowl. Add sugar mixture to cherry juices in skillet and simmer, stirring, until thickened, about 3 minutes. Stir cherry sauce and vanilla into cherries and cool.

Line lower rack of oven with foil and preheat oven to 400 degrees.

Gourmet July 1997, R.S.V P. Cassis Bistro, Seattle, Washington

On a lightly floured surface with a floured rolling pin roll out 1 piece of dough into an 11-inch round (about $1/8$-inch thick). Fit dough into a 9-inch (1-quart) pie plate, leaving a $3/4$-inch overhang. Pour filling into shell and chill, loosely covered with plastic wrap.

On a lightly floured surface roll out remaining dough into an 11-inch round (about $1/8$-inch thick) and with a sharp knife or fluted pastry wheel cut into 1-inch-wide strips. Working on a sheet of wax paper set on a baking sheet, weave pastry strips in a close lattice pattern. Chill or freeze lattice on wax paper on a flat surface 20 minutes, or until firm. Brush edge of filled shell with cold water and slide lattice off wax paper and onto pie. Let lattice stand 10 minutes to soften. Trim edges flush with rim of pie plate and crimp decoratively. Gently brush lattice top with cold water and sprinkle with sugar.

Bake pie in middle of oven 45 minutes, or until pastry is golden and filling just begins to bubble, and transfer to a rack to cool slightly. Serve pie warm with ice cream.

Makes one pie.

Tapawingo's Molten Chocolate Cakes with Cherries

1 16-ounce bag frozen pitted dark
    sweet **cherries**, halved,
    thawed, undrained
$3/4$ cup sugar
$1/4$ cup kirsch (clear cherry brandy)
    or regular brandy
$1/4$ teaspoon ground cinnamon

2 tablespoons unsweetened cocoa
    powder
2 ounces bittersweet
    (not unsweetened) or semi
    sweet chocolate, chopped
$1/4$ cup ($1/2$ stick) unsalted butter, cut
    into small pieces
2 large egg yolks
1 large egg
2 teaspoons all purpose flour

Powdered sugar
Fresh mint

Preheat oven to 350 degrees.

Combine cherries with juices, $1/2$ cup sugar, kirsch, and cinnamon in heavy medium saucepan. Stir over medium heat until sugar dissolves. Simmer until sauce thickens and is slightly reduced, about 10 minutes. Using slotted spoon, remove $1/4$ cup cherries from sauce; drain well. Transfer to work surface and chop coarsely; reserve chopped cherries for cakes. Set aside cherry sauce. Butter two $3/4$ cup ramekins or custard cups. Whisk cocoa and remaining $1/4$ cup sugar in small bowl to blend. Stir chocolate and butter in heavy small saucepan over low heat until chocolate melts. Remove from heat; whisk in cocoa mixture. Whisk in egg yolks, then whole egg and flour. Fold in reserved $1/4$ cup chopped cherries. Divide batter between prepared ramekins. (Sauce and cake batter can be made 1 day ahead. Cover separately; chill.) Bake cakes uncovered until edges are set but center is still shiny and tester inserted into center comes out with some wet batter attached, about 22 minutes. Warm sauce over low heat. Cut around cakes to loosen; turn out onto plates. Spoon sauce alongside. Sift powdered sugar over; garnish with mint.

Makes two servings.

Tapawingo, Ellsworth, Michigan

Dried Cherry-Chocolate Strudel Bars

2 cups all-purpose flour
$^1/_2$ cup (1 stick) unsalted butter, room
    temperature
$^1/_4$ teaspoon salt
$^1/_2$ cup sour cream

1 $^1/_2$ cups cherry jam
2 cups (about 10 ounces) almonds,
    toasted, finely chopped
1 cup dried tart cherries
1 cup mini-semisweet chocolate chips
    (about 6 ounces)

Using on/off turns, blend first 3 ingredients in processor until coarse meal forms. Add sour cream and process just until moist clumps form. Gather dough into ball; divide in half. Flatten each dough piece into a thin rectangle. Wrap in plastic and chill until firm enough to roll, at least 30 minutes and up to 2 days.

Preheat oven to 350 degrees. Line baking sheet with parchment paper. Roll out 1 dough piece on lightly floured surface to 14x12-inch rectangle. Leaving 1-inch plain border at 1 long side, spread with $^3/_4$ cup cherry jam, then sprinkle with 1 cup almonds, $^1/_2$ cup dried cherries and $^1/_2$ cup chocolate chips. Starting opposite plain end, roll up dough jelly-roll style, enclosing filling. Push in ends to compress log to 12-inch length; seal ends. Transfer strudel, seam side down, to prepared baking sheet. Repeat with remaining dough and filling, spacing strudels evenly apart on baking sheet.

Bake strudels until golden, about 1 hour 20 minutes. Slide spatula under hot strudels to loosen from sheet. Cool completely on sheet. Cut strudels crosswise into $^3/_4$-inch-thick bars. (Store airtight at room temperature up to 3 days.)

Makes twenty-four

Leslie Berman, Skokie, Illinois in *Bon Appetit* February 2001

Pumpkin Cake
With Sage Ice Cream and Pumpkin-Cherry Compote

For sage ice cream:
2 cups heavy cream
2 cups half-and-half
$^1/_3$ cup coarsely chopped fresh sage
4 (2 by $^1/_2$-inch) strips lemon zest
9 large egg yolks
$^3/_4$ cup granulated sugar
$^1/_4$ teaspoon salt

For pumpkin cake:
$2^1/_4$ cups all-purpose flour
$1^1/_2$ teaspoons cinnamon
$1^1/_2$ teaspoons ground allspice
1 teaspoon baking soda
$^1/_2$ teaspoon salt
$1^3/_4$ cups packed light brown sugar
4 large eggs
1 cup safflower or canola oil
$1^1/_2$ cups canned pumpkin

For compote:
$^1/_2$ cup dried tart cherries
2 tablespoons unsalted butter
$^1/_2$ cup packed light brown sugar
$^1/_4$ cup granulated sugar
2 tablespoons fresh lemon juice
$^1/_4$ teaspoon cinnamon
$^1/_8$ teaspoon salt
2 cups fresh pumpkin, in $^1/_4$-inch dice

Equipment needed: Instant-read thermometer and ice cream maker.

Make ice cream:
Bring cream, half-and-half, sage, and zest to a boil in a large heavy saucepan over moderate heat. Remove from heat and steep, covered, 10 minutes.

Whisk together yolks, granulated sugar, and salt in a large bowl. Whisk in half of hot cream, then whisk egg mixture into remaining cream in saucepan. Cook custard over moderate heat, stirring constantly with a wooden spoon, until it coats back of spoon and reaches 170 degrees on thermometer, about 5 minutes (do not let boil).

Pour custard through a fine sieve into a bowl and cool, stirring occasionally. Chill custard, its surface covered with plastic wrap, until cold, at least 3 hours.

Freeze custard in ice cream maker, then transfer to an airtight container and put in freezer to harden.

For cake:
Preheat oven to 350 degrees.

Butter a 13 x 9 x 2 inch metal baking pan. Line bottom with wax or parchment paper, then butter paper. Sift together flour, cinnamon, allspice, baking soda and salt. Whisk together brown sugar and eggs in a large bowl, then whisk in oil and pumpkin purée. Add flour mixture and whisk just until smooth. Pour batter into baking pan and bake in middle of oven until springy to the touch and a tester inserted in center comes out clean, 25 to 30 minutes. Cool cake in pan on a rack 10 minutes, then run a knife around edge and invert onto rack. Peel off paper and cool cake completely.

For compote:
Soak cherries in hot water to cover until softened, about 15 minutes, then drain.
Melt butter in a large skillet over moderate heat. Add sugars, lemon juice, cinnamon and salt, then cook, stirring until smooth. Add pumpkin and drained cherries and simmer, covered, stirring occasionally, until pumpkin is tender, 8 to 12 minutes.

Assemble dessert:
Cut out 12 (3-inch) rounds from cake with cutter. Halve each round horizontally, then put bottom halves on 12 plates and top with scoops of ice cream. Spoon compote on and around cakes, then tilt tops against ice cream.

Note: Custard can be chilled up to 24 hours before making ice cream.
Pumpkin cake and sage ice cream keep, frozen separately, 1 month. Wrap cake tightly in plastic wrap and foil. Thaw cake (in wrapping) at room temperature.

Makes twelve servings

Adapted from pastry chef Elissa Narow, Blackbird, Chicago, Illinois-*Gourmet* October 2001.

Cherry Apple Crisp

3 cups peeled and chopped apples

2 cups fresh **cherries**, pitted

$1/2$ cup plus 2 tablespoons
    all-purpose flour

1 cup granulated sugar

3 packages instant oatmeal with
    cinnamon and spice

$3/4$ cup pecans, chopped

$1/2$ cup firmly packed brown sugar

8 tablespoons butter (1 stick), melted

Pecan halves and fresh pitted
    cherries for garnish

Preheat oven to 350 degrees.

Combine the apples, cherries and 2 tablespoons of the flour, toss to coat. Add the granulated sugar and mix well. Place in a 2-quart casserole. Combine the oatmeal, pecans, $1/2$ cup flour and brown sugar. Add butter and stir well. Spoon over the fruit mixture and bake uncovered for 45 minutes. Garnish with pecan halves and cherries. Serve with ice cream.

Serves eight

Adapted from *The Junior League Centennial Cookbook*

Tapawingo's Cherry Ice Cream

4 large eggs
1^1/2 cups sugar
1 cup **cherry** brandy
^{1}/4 cup kirsch
6 cups half and half
^{1}/2 cup fresh chopped black cherries

Equipment needed: ice cream maker.

Whip eggs and sugar in electric mixer; set aside. Place brandy and kirsch in saucepan and heat to burn off alcohol, then cool.

Add half and half to egg mixture. Add liqueur to base, freeze according to ice cream freezer's manufacturers instructions.

Fold in chopped cherries.

Tapawingo, Ellsworth, Michigan

Marion Kane's Oatmeal Cherry Chocolate Chippers

$^3/4$ cup butter, at room temperature

$^3/4$ cup packed brown sugar

$^1/4$ cup granulated sugar

1 egg

2 teaspoons vanilla

1 tablespoon water

$^3/4$ cup all-purpose flour

$^3/4$ teaspoon baking soda

Pinch salt

2 cups quick-cooking (not instant) rolled oats

1 cup crisp rice cereal

1 cup dried cherries

1 cup semi-sweet chocolate chips or chopped semi-sweet chocolate

Preheat oven to 350 degrees.

In large bowl, using electric mixer on medium speed, cream butter, sugars, egg, vanilla and water until light and creamy.

In small bowl, combine flour, baking soda and salt. Add to creamed mixture, beating on low speed until blended. With wooden spoon, stir in oats and rice cereal, then dried cherries and chocolate.

Using an ice cream scoop or round spoon, place balls of dough on Silpat- or parchment paper-lined cookie sheet about 2 inches apart. Flatten each ball with fingers until cookies are about $1/2$-inch thick. Bake 12 to 15 minutes or until golden brown. Cool a few minutes before transferring to rack to cool completely.

Makes about thirty cookies

Marion Kane, *Toronto Star* food columnist

130

NATIONAL CHERRY FESTIVAL

TRAVERSE CITY, MICHIGAN

NATIONAL CHERRY QUEEN

The first Cherry Blossom Parade in 1925 assembed horseback riders, marching bands, and THE QUEEN, selected by pulling a name out of a hat. The parade wound around Traverse City's downtown for the coronation and then went around the downtown again just for good measure.

Tapawingo's Tart Cherry-Maple Pie

Pastry:

1 cup unbleached flour

1/2 cup whole wheat pastry flour

2 ounces blanched almonds, roasted, and finely ground

1/2 teaspoon ground cinnamon

4 ounces unsalted butter, chilled and cubed

3 tablespoons pure maple syrup

1 egg yolk

1 scant teaspoon grated lemon zest

Filling:

4 cups fresh tart cherries, pitted (about 2 pounds). Save all juice in pitting process

2 tablespoons quick-cooking tapioca

2 tablespoons cornstarch

3/4 cup maple syrup

1/2 teaspoon cinnamon

1 tablespoon lemon juice

1 teaspoon grated lemon zest

Pastry:

In the food processor, combine the flours, ground almonds, cinnamon and butter. Pulse the machine until the mixture resembles coarse meal. Add the maple syrup, egg yolk and lemon zest, and pulse again, until the dough just starts to form a mass. Remove from processor bowl, form into a compact disc, wrap in plastic wrap and chill for 1/2 hour. Roll the dough, between sheets of parchment or plastic film, into a circle large enough to fit into the 10-inch pie pan. (Nut dough is fragile and cannot be rolled much thinner than 3/16 to 1/4- inch thickness.) Make a decorative rim.

Chill for an additional 15 minutes. Line the shell with parchment and pie weights (or dried beans) and bake in a preheated 375-degree oven for 10 minutes. Remove the lining, and bake for an additional 7 to 10 minutes, until the crust crisps and browns. Remove to a rack to cool.

Combine the cherries and their juice, tapioca, cornstarch, syrup, and cinnamon in a non-reactive saucepan. Let sit for about 15 minutes, until the cherries have released more juices and the tapioca has softened. Place pan over medium

Maple Meringue:
1 cup pure maple syrup
4 large egg whites, at room
      temperature
1 teaspoon lemon juice
1 teaspoon vanilla

heat and slowly bring to a boil, stirring occasionally. Cook till the filling has thickened and the tapioca is clear. Be careful not to break-up cherries. Take off heat and stir in lemon juice and lemon zest. Pour into baked pastry shell.

For Meringue:
Preheat oven to 400 degrees.
Place the maple syrup in a small pan. Bring to boil and cook until syrup comes to a soft-ball stage, or about 238 degrees. Meanwhile, beat the egg whites till soft peaks form. Immediately, pour the syrup into the whites in a thread-like stream. Beat until the meringue is firm and shiny, 2 or 3 more minutes. Fold in the lemon juice and vanilla, and spoon meringue into a large pastry bag with a large star tip. Pipe towering, generous mounds on the cherry filling, one for each piece, and one in the center. Place pie on a cookie sheet and place in 400 degree oven for 5 to 7 minutes, or until ridges in meringue are nicely browned. Let pie return to room temperature before serving

Note: About one half of the meringue is needed if you choose to pipe on a lattice-type topping.

Makes one ten-inch pie

Tapawingo, Ellsworth, Michigan

Keith Famie's Autumn Apple Bake

4 Granny Smith Apples
$1/2$ cup raisins, chopped fine
1 teaspoon ground cinnamon
2 cups pecans, chopped fine
1 cup brown sugar
$1/2$ cup dried cherries, chopped fine
$1/2$ cup butter
5 6x6 sheets puff pastry
2 egg whites for wash
whipped cream for topping

Preheat oven to 400 degrees.

Peel apples and completely hollow out the apple core with a melon baller. Mix the remaining ingredients (with exception of puff pastry, egg whites and whipped cream) together with a spoon or in a food processor. The mixture will have a paste appearance. Fill apples from both ends with the mixture.

Wrap each apple in a sheet of puff pastry. With a small paring knife, cut the excess dough in the shape of leaves and decorate the tops of the apples with two leaves.

Egg wash the puff pastry and bake until golden brown. Top with fresh whipped cream.

Serves four

Keith Famie's Adventures in Cooking

Carol Haddix's Double Cherry Lemon Pie

For the pastry:
2 1/2 cups flour
Zest of 1 lemon
1 tablespoon sugar
Dash salt
2 sticks (1 cup) butter, chilled, cut into
    pieces
1/4 cup vegetable shortening
6 to 8 tablespoons ice water

For the filling:
1 cup dried tart cherries
2 tablespoons dry red wine
Zest of 1 lemon
1 1/2 tablespoons cornstarch
2 cans (14 1/2 ounces each) tart
    cherries in water, drained,
    juice reserved
1/2 cup sugar
2 tablespoons butter

This pie uses two types of cherries, canned and dried, as well as lemon zest in the filling and in the crust. It is quite tart; if you prefer sweeter pies, increase the sugar to 3/4 cup.

Heat oven to 425 degrees.

Mix flour, lemon zest, sugar and salt together in food processor. Add butter pieces and shortening; pulse to work butter in until texture of peas. Add 6 tablespoons of the ice water; pulse until mixture begins to gather together, adding more water if needed. Remove; form into two balls. Cover with plastic wrap; chill for at least 30 minutes. Meanwhile, for filling, mix dried cherries with red wine, lemon, cornstarch and 1/2 cup of the reserved cherry juice in large bowl. Stir in cornstarch. Let marinate 30 minutes; stir. Add canned cherries to dried cherry mixture. Stir in sugar.

Roll out one ball of pastry to fit 9-inch pie pan. Fit into pan. Fill with cherry mixture. Dot with butter. Roll out remaining pastry. Cut decorative designs in pastry, if desired. Fit over top of cherry filling. Fold edge of top crust under edge of bottom crust. Flute pastry.

Place pie on a cookie sheet. Bake 15 minutes. Reduce oven temperature to 350 degrees. Bake until crust is golden brown and filling is bubbling, about 45 minutes. Cool at least 30 minutes.

Makes one pie

Carol Mighton Haddix, food editor, *Chicago Tribune*

"Cherries, ripe cherries!"
The old woman cried,
In her snowy white apron,
And basket beside;

And the little boys came,
Eyes shining, cheeks red,
To buy bags of cherries
To eat with their bread.

—Walter de la Mare

Keith Famie's Michigan Apple and Cherry Cobbler

1 1/2 pounds butter
1 1/2 cups brown sugar
2 cinnamon sticks
8 Granny Smith apples, peeled, cored,
    and diced
1 1/2 cups dried cherries
1/2 cup brandy
3 sheets pie dough or puff pastry
1 egg, beaten lightly for egg wash
whipped cream for topping

Preheat oven to 400 degrees

In a saute' pan, melt butter with brown sugar and cinnamon. Stir in apples, cherries, and brandy. Cook over medium heat for 10 minutes, stirring occasionally until apples are soft. Remove the mixture from heat and cool to room temperature. This can be made a day ahead and refrigerated.

Fill 4 individual dishes or 9x9-inch glass or ceramic dish to the top with the apple mixture. Place pie dough on top, being sure that you cover all of the mixture. Brush lightly with egg wash.

Bake in oven for 15 to 20 minutes or until the top is golden brown. Serve with fresh whipped cream.

Serve four

Keith Famie's Adventures in Cooking

Keith Famie's Michigan Bread Pudding

Pudding:

3 tablespoons butter

2 Granny Smith apples, peeled, cored and cubed

1 teaspoon vanilla

1 $1/2$ teaspoons cinnamon

1 cup brown sugar

1 cup dried cherries

$1/2$ teaspoon nutmeg

$1/4$ teaspoon ground cloves

$3/4$ cup Maker's Mark bourbon

2 cups heavy cream

3 eggs, lightly beaten

2 egg yolks, lightly beaten

6 to 7 cups small bread cubes, crusts removed. Use brioche, French bread, wheat or cinnamon

Michigan Maple Crème Anglaise recipe on facing page

Preheat oven to 375 degrees.

Butter an 8x8-inch baking pan with 1 tablespoon of the butter. Set aside. In large skillet, melt remaining butter, add cubed apples and saute' for about 3 minutes. Stir in vanilla, cinnamon, brown sugar, dried cherries, nutmeg, cloves and bourbon. Continue to cook until the apples are tender but hold their shape, about 5 to 7 minutes. Remove from heat and set aside to cool. In a medium bowl, mix together heavy cream, eggs, and egg yolks until well blended. In a separate large bowl, mix together the bread cubes and sauteed apple mixture. Add half of the egg mixture and mix thoroughly. Spoon bread mixture into buttered loaf pan and pour the remaining custard over the top. Place the baking dish into a larger pan, about 2 inches deep. Pour warm water into the larger pan, to a depth about halfway up the outside of the baking dish. Bake the pudding for 45 minutes to 1 hour, or until the custard puffs up slightly and is lightly browned. During the last 35 minutes of baking, cover with foil. Remove from oven and let cool for 10 minutes. Spoon the pudding onto serving plates, drizzle with the Michigan Maple Crème Anglaise and serve.

Keith Famie's Michigan Maple Crème Anglaise

1 cup milk
1/4 cup heavy whipping cream
1 vanilla bean, split and scraped of
      seeds, or 1 teaspoon vanilla
      extract
4 large egg yolks
1/4 cup sugar
1/2 cup maple syrup

In the top of a double boiler, bring the milk, cream, and vanilla to a boil, stirring constantly. Reduce the heat and simmer for 3 to 4 minutes. In a medium bowl, whisk together the egg yolks and sugar. Stir 1/4 cup of the warm milk mixture into the egg mixture. Then, pour the entire egg mixture into the double boiler mixture. Mix thoroughly over medium to low heat for 4 minutes, stirring constantly until the mixture lightly coats the back of a wooden spoon.

Remove the sauce from the heat and strain it into a medium bowl, using a mesh strainer to remove any particles of cooked egg. Whisk in the maple syrup in a steady stream.

Drizzle on top of Michigan Bread Pudding, recipe on facing page.

Keith Famie's Adventures in Cooking

Tapawingo's Chocolate-Cherry Biscotti

1^1/2 cups all-purpose flour
^{1}/2 cup unsweetened cocoa powder
1 teaspoon baking powder
^{1}/2 teaspoon salt
2 large eggs
1 cup sugar
1 teaspoon pure vanilla extract
1 cup dried sour cherries

Preheat the oven to 350 degrees.

Line a cookie sheet with parchment paper. In a medium bowl, sift together the flour, cocoa, baking powder and salt. In a large bowl, using an electric mixer, beat the eggs, sugar and vanilla until very pale and thick, about 3 minutes. Stir in the dry ingredients, then the cherries; the dough will be stiff.

Divide the dough in half. With damp hands, shape each half into a smooth, 12-inch log on the prepared cookie sheet. Bake for about 30 minutes, or until the loaves spring back when lightly touched in the center.

Carefully transfer the logs to a cutting board. Using a serrated knife and a gentle sawing motion, slice the logs diagonally crosswise, ^{3}/4-inch thick. Stand the biscotti on a baking sheet ^{1}/2-inch apart. Bake for about 10 minutes, or until crisp. Transfer to a wire rack to cool.

Makes about thirty-six cookies

Tapawingo, Ellsworth, Michigan

Baklava with Cherries

Pastry:

4 cups almonds, walnuts or equal
    parts of both, coarsely
    chopped

$3/4$ cup sugar

1 tablespoon ground cinnamon

$1/4$ teaspoon ground cloves

$1/4$ cup dried cherries, chopped

$1/2$ pound clarified unsalted butter,
    melted

1 pound phyllo dough, thawed in the
    refrigerator if frozen

Lemon syrup:

2 cups water

2 cups sugar

2 lemon zest strips, each 3 inches long

2 tablespoons fresh lemon juice

Preheat oven to 350 degrees.

In a bowl, combine nuts, sugar, cinnamon, cloves and cherries. Lightly brush a 9 x 14 x 2-inch baking pan with some of the melted butter.

Lay phyllo sheets flat on a work surface. Cover with a damp towel or plastic wrap to prevent them from drying out. Lay a phyllo sheet in the prepared pan and brush it lightly with butter. Working with 1 sheet at a time, top with half of the remaining phyllo sheets, (10-12 sheets, brushing each with butter after it is placed in the pan. Spread the nut mixture evenly over the stacked phyllo sheets, again brushing each sheet lightly with butter, including the top sheet. Cover and refrigerate about 30 minutes so the butter will set. Using a sharp knife, cut the baklava all the way through into diamond shapes, forming about 36 pieces in all. Bake until golden brown, 35 to 40 minutes.

Lemon syrup:

In a deep saucepan, combine water, sugar and lemon zest and bring to a boil. Reduce heat to low and simmer until thickened, about 15 minutes. Remove lemon zest and discard. Add lemon juice. Pour over just baked baklava, recut diamonds. Let stand for 30 minutes before serving.

Adapted from *Taverna*

Makes thirty-six pieces

Kate Lawson's Cherry-Apple Crumble

1 pound fresh tart cherries, pitted and rinsed
1 1/2 cups sugar
3 tablespoons cornstarch
3 apples peeled, cored and sliced
Juice and grated zest of 1 orange
1 stick cold, unsalted butter, cut up
3/4 cup brown sugar
1 teaspoon cinnamon
3/4 cup old-fashioned rolled oats
3/4 cup flour

Preheat oven to 375 degrees.

Butter a 9-inch baking dish. Stir together half the cherries, sugar and cornstarch in saucepan. Bring to a boil, remove from heat. Add the remaining cherries, apples, orange juice and zest. Pour the mixture into the prepared dish.

In food processor cut the butter, sugar, cinnamon, oatmeal and flour together until it crumbles. Spread over the fruit and place in oven. Bake until top is brown and filling is bubbly, about 35 minutes.

Serves six to eight

Kate Lawson, *Detroit News* food columnist

Cherry-Vanilla Tea Cakes

1¹/2 cups all-purpose flour
1 teaspoon baking powder
¹/2 teaspoon baking soda
¹/4 teaspoon salt
¹/8 teaspoon ground nutmeg
¹/2 cup (1 stick) unsalted butter, room
  temperature
1 cup plus 1 tablespoon sugar
2 large eggs, room temperature
2 teaspoons vanilla extract
²/3 cup sour cream
1 teaspoon grated lemon peel
1 cup canned pitted sweet cherries,
  halved, drained
¹/2 vanilla bean, split lengthwise
2 tablespoons powdered sugar

Preheat oven to 350 degrees.

Lightly butter and flour 10-inch springform pan. Sift first 5 ingredients into medium bowl. Using electric mixer, beat butter and 1 cup sugar in large bowl until well blended. Add eggs 1 at a time, beating well after each addition. Blend in vanilla extract. Transfer 2 tablespoons dry ingredients to a small bowl. On low speed, beat half of remaining dry ingredients into butter mixture, then mix in sour cream and lemon peel. Beat in remaining half of dry ingredients. Mix cherries into reserved 2 tablespoons dry ingredients; fold cherries into batter. Spoon batter into prepared pan; smooth top with spoon. Bake until tester inserted into center of cake comes out clean, about 30 minutes. Transfer cake to rack and cool 10 minutes. Meanwhile, using a small sharp knife, scrape seeds from vanilla bean into small bowl. Mix in 1 tablespoon sugar, rubbing with fingertips to distribute seeds. Add powdered sugar and rub again. Sift vanilla sugar over hot cake and cool. Cut around pan sides to loosen cake; remove pan sides. (Can be made 1 day ahead. Cover; let stand at room temperature.)

Serves ten

Ken Haedrich in *Bon Appetit*

Jimmy Schmidt's Sour Cherry Tart

Tart shell:
1/2 cup hazelnuts, toasted and skinned
1/2 cup confectioners' sugar
3/4 pound (3 sticks) unsalted
       butter
1 large egg
2 tablespoons grated orange rind
1/4 teaspoon salt
2 cups pastry flour

Filling:
1/2 cup sugar
2 large eggs, lightly beaten
2 large egg yolks
1 teaspoon vanilla extract
Pinch of salt
1/2 cup of half and half, scalded

1 cup pepper vodka
4 tablespoons (1/2 stick) unsalted butter
3 cups sour cherries, pitted
Confectioners' sugar for dusting

Tart Shell:

In a food processor, grind the nuts and sugar together until fine. Add the butter and whip until light. Add the egg, orange rind and salt. Add the flour, mixing until just combined. Transfer the dough to a piece of parchment or wax paper and flatten into a disc. Cover with another piece of parchment, and refrigerate until firm, at least 8 hours. Dust the dough with flour, then roll the dough out between sheets of parchment to a thickness of 1/4-inch. Fit into an 11-inch tart pan, trim, and finish edges. Refrigerate at least 30 minutes before baking. Keep pastry cool for easy handling.

For the filling:
Preheat the oven to 375 degrees.
Line the tart shell with foil, shiny-side down. Fill with pie weights or dried beans, then bake until set, about 20 minutes. Remove the beans and foil and continue baking until browned, about 15 minutes.
In a medium-sized bowl, combine the sugar, eggs, egg yolks, vanilla and salt. Add the hot half-and-half, then the vodka. Strain through a fine

Makes one 11-inch tart

sieve. In a large skillet over high heat, melt the butter, then add the cherries. Cook until the cherries are warm and the juices have thickened enough to coat the fruit, about 5 minutes.

To assemble:
Spoon the cherries into the tart shell, then pour in the custard. Bake until the custard sets, about 10 minutes. Cool on a rack. Dust the tart with confectioners' sugar, then serve.

Sour Cherry Mooss

4 cups fresh or frozen pitted sour
    cherries
5 $1/2$ cups sugar
$1/2$ cup flour
$1/2$ teaspoon salt
3 cups milk
$1/2$ teaspoon almond extract
several drops of red food coloring,
    optional

Put the cherries and 4 cups of the sugar in a large saucepan. Pour in 1 cup of water, bring to a boil, reduce the heat, and simmer uncovered, until some of the cherry skins crack, about 10 minutes. Meanwhile, combine $1/2$ cup of the sugar, the flour, and the salt in a medium bowl. Add the milk, and whisk until the mixture has a gravy-like consistency.

When the cherry skins have begun cracking, stir in the remaining 1 cup of sugar.

Increase the heat to medium-high and whisk in the flour-milk mixture.

Whisk constantly until the mooss comes to a boil and the liquid coats the back of a spoon. Remove from the heat and whisk in the almond extract and, if you like, the food coloring.

Transfer to a serving bowl and serve warm, or refrigerate, covered, to serve chilled.

Serves eight to twelve

Prairie Home Cooking

Bittersweet Chocolate Cake With Dried Cherries

7 ounces bittersweet
      (not unsweetened) or semi-
      sweet chocolate, chopped
1/2 cup (1 stick) unsalted butter,
      diced
1 cup dried tart cherries (about 5
      ounces), coarsely chopped
1/2 cup framboise eau-de-vie (clear
      raspberry brandy)

1 cup sugar
1 teaspoon vanilla extract
1/4 teaspoon salt
4 large eggs
2/3 cup all-purpose flour

Powdered sugar

Preheat oven to 350 degrees.

Position rack in center of oven. Line bottom of 9-inch round cake pan with 2-inch-high sides with parchment paper. Generously butter and flour sides of pan and parchment. Stir chocolate and butter in large bowl set over saucepan of simmering water until melted and smooth. Turn off heat. Let chocolate stand over water. Mix cherries and framboise in medium saucepan. Bring to simmer over medium heat. Reduce heat to low; simmer until all liquid is absorbed, stirring often, about 9 minutes. Set aside.

Remove bowl with melted chocolate from over water. Whisk in sugar, vanilla and salt, then eggs 1 at a time. Add flour in 2 additions, blending well after each. Fold in cherries. Pour batter into pan. Bake cake until tester inserted into center comes out with moist crumbs attached, about 35 minutes. Cool completely in pan on rack. Cut around pan sides to loosen cake. Turn out cake onto plate; peel off parchment paper. (Can be prepared 2 days ahead. Store airtight at room temperature.) Sift powdered sugar generously over cake.

Makes twelve servings.

Bon Appétit February 2001

Sauteed Cherries

2 pounds fat, juicy **cherries**, pitted
2 tablespoons unsalted butter
2 tablespoons light brown sugar
Freshly squeezed lemon juice
8 ounces top-quality vanilla ice cream

Melt the butter in a medium skillet over medium heat. Add the sugar, stir, then add the cherries and cook, stirring occasionally, until the cherries are tender and hot through, about 3-5 minutes. Add the lemon juice, stir, then remove from the heat. Divide the cherries among 6 shallow dishes, and serve with vanilla ice cream.

Makes four to six servings.

Letter from France, July 2000, Susan Hermann Loomis, *Bon Appetit*

My baby loves me, yes, yes, she does
All other girls outta sight
Says she loves me, yes, yes she does
She's gonna show me the night

She got the way to move me Cherry
She got the way to groove me
Cherry baby now
She got the way to groove me
Alright
She got the way to groove me

—*Cherry, Cherry* by Neil Diamond, 1966

Tapawingo's Chocolate Bread and Butter Pudding with Michigan Tart Cherries

Pudding:
4 ounces unsalted butter
10 ounces brioche, cut into 1-inch squares
2 cups heavy cream
1 cup milk
6 ounces bittersweet chocolate, finely
      chopped
8 egg yolks
2/3 cup packed brown sugar
pinch salt
1 teaspoon pure vanilla extract
1 cup, or more, dried tart cherries

Vanilla Custard Sauce:
1 1/2 cups light cream
1 vanilla bean
1/4 cup sugar
Pinch of salt
3 egg yolks

In a large saute' pan, melt the butter and toss the brioche cubes until they are very lightly toasted. Remove from heat and pour cubes into a large mixing bowl.

In a 2-quart nonreactive pan heat the cream and milk, almost to the boil. Remove from heat and immediately stir in the chocolate, stirring occasionally until the chocolate is fully melted. Reserve.

Preheat oven to 325 degrees. Mix together the egg yolks, brown sugar, vanilla and salt, until well blended, but not frothy. Slowly pour warm chocolate mixture into egg mixture and stir until well blended. Strain this chocolate custard over brioche cubes, stir in the dried tart cherries, and cover with a small plate to keep the cubes submerged. Let stand for one hour so the brioche absorbs the liquid. Remove plate and spoon mixture into 8 individual, souffle-style baking dishes. Place dishes into a large baking pan filled halfway with hot water. Cover pan with foil, punched with a few holes to let steam escape. Bake at 325 degrees for about 60 minutes, or till the custard has set and the top has a dark rich chocolate color. Serve pudding slightly warm with heavy cream or vanilla custard sauce. (recipe follows).

Tapawingo, Ellsworth, Michigan

For Vanilla Custard Sauce:

Split the vanilla bean lengthwise and scrape out seeds. Place all the bean pod, the seeds and the cream in a heavy, nonreactive saucepan, and bring just to the boiling point over low heat. Beat the sugar, salt, and egg yolks in a bowl until smooth and lemon colored. Pour a little of the hot cream into the egg mixture, then return everything to saucepan. Over low heat, stir with a wooden spoon until mixture coats the back of the spoon. Do not allow it to boil or the egg yolks will curdle. Take off heat, removing the vanilla bean pod, cool and refrigerate.

—

Makes eight servings

Cherry Tiramisu

1 cup Italian-style ricotta cheese
1 cup confectioners' sugar
$1/4$ cup sour cream
$1/4$ cup coffee liqueur
$1^1/2$ cups shortbread cookie crumbs
    (about 30 2-inch cookies)
1 21-ounce can cherry pie filling
grated chocolate, for garnish
fresh mint leaves, for garnish

In a large mixing bowl, combine ricotta cheese, confectioners' sugar, sour cream and coffee liqueur; mix well. Set aside.

In an electric blender or food processor container, process cookies, in small batches, until finely crushed. Remove 6 cherries from cherry pie filling; reserve for garnish.

To assemble dessert, spoon two tablespoons ricotta cheese mixture into each of six (8-ounce) parfait glasses. Add 2 tablespoons cookie crumbs to each glass; top each with 2 tablespoons of cherry pie filling. Repeat ricotta, crumb and cherry layers. Finish each serving with an equal portion of the remaining ricotta cheese mixture.

Garnish with reserved cherries, grated chocolate and mint leaves, if desired. Let chill 2 to 3 hours before serving.

Serves six

Cherry Marketing Institute

Dried Cherry Upside-Down Cake

2 cups dried tart cherries
1/4 cup dark Jamaican rum
1 cup (2 sticks) butter,
    at room temperature
3/4 cup brown sugar, firmly packed
1 cup walnut or pecan halves
1/4 teaspoon ground cinnamon
1/4 teaspoon salt
1 cup confectioners' sugar
2 egg yolks
1 whole egg
3/4 teaspoon vanilla extract
3/4 cup unsifted cake flour
unsweetened whipped cream

Preheat the oven to 325 degrees.

Cover the cherries with 2 cups of very hot tap water and let stand 45 minutes. Drain, pressing gently; the cherries should seem plump and moist but not sodden. Return the cherries to their soaking bowl, add the rum, and stir. Let stand for 30 to 60 minutes, stirring several times.

Melt 1 stick of the butter in a 9-inch cast iron skillet. Remove from the heat and stir in the brown sugar. Sprinkle the cherries and their liquid on top, making a fairly even layer, then distribute the nuts over the cherries, pressing them down lightly. Sprinkle with cinnamon and set aside.

With an electric mixer, beat the remaining 1/2 cup of butter and salt for 3 minutes at high speed. Add the confectioners' sugar gradually and beat 3 minutes longer. Add the egg yolks one at a time and beat for 2 full minutes longer after the last has gone in. Add the whole egg and vanilla and beat only until the mixture looks smooth and creamy. Sprinkle or sift the flour on top and fold it in gently.

Heartland: The Best of the Old and the New from Midwest Kitchens

Spread the cake batter evenly over the cherries and bake for 30 to 40 minutes, or until the top is browned and a cake tester inserted in the center of the cake comes out clean. Let the cake stand for 3 minutes after removing from the oven, then run a knife around the sides and invert onto a serving platter. Serve warm or at room temperature, with whipped cream on the side.

Makes 1 cake

Sour Cherry Pie

Filling:

1 recipe Flaky Pie Crust or other
      pastry for two 9-inch pie crusts

1 cup plus 1 teaspoon sugar

3 tablespoons instant tapioca

1 tablespoon lemon juice

$1/2$ teaspoon almond extract

4 cups sour cherries, pitted

1 tablespoon unsalted butter,
      cut into dots

2 tablespoons milk or light cream

Flaky Pie Crust:

2 cups all-purpose flour

$1/2$ teaspoon salt

$1/2$ cup lard or shortening, chilled

2 tablespoons unsalted butter, chilled

6 tablespoons milk, chilled

Preheat the oven to 425 degrees.

Roll out the pastry to make 2 crusts and place one of them in a 9-inch pie pan.

Stir together the 1 cup sugar and the tapioca, lemon juice and almond extract in a large bowl. Add the sour cherries and toss gently to coat the fruit. Spoon the mixture into the pie pan and dot the top with the butter. Wet your fingertips with water and moisten the exposed edges of the crust. Cover with the top crust and crimp or flute the edges together. Cut several steam vents in the top crust. Brush the top crust with the milk and sprinkle with the 1 teaspoon sugar.

Bake the pie for 15 minutes, reduce the heat to 350 degrees, and bake for 45 to 55 minutes more, or until the cherries are tender, the filling has thickened, and the crust is golden brown. Transfer to rack to cool, and serve.

Makes one pie

Prairie Home Cooking

Flaky pie crust: Stir together the flour and salt in a mixing bowl. With a pastry blender or two knives, cut in the lard or shortening and butter until the mixture resembles coarse meal.

Using a fork, blend in the milk 1 tablespoon at a time. Pat down the dough with your hands and form it into a ball. Divide the dough in half, and wrap each half in plastic wrap. Refrigerate the dough for a least 30 minutes before using it in a recipe. Before rolling out the dough, let it rest at room temperature for 15 minutes; this step prevents cracking.

Makes one pie

Baked Cherry Dumplings

4 cups tart red cherries, washed and
   pitted
1 cup plus 2 tablespoons granulated
   sugar
1/4 cup brown sugar
2 tablespoons quick-cooking tapioca
1/2 teaspoon almond extract
1 1/2 cups all-purpose flour
2 teaspoons baking powder
1/2 teaspoon salt
6 tablespoons (3/4 stick) cold butter
1 egg
1/3 cup milk
1/2 teaspoon grated nutmeg

Preheat the oven to 400 degrees.

In a shallow 2-quart casserole or 12 x 7-inch pan, combine the cherries, 1 cup of granulated sugar, the brown sugar, tapioca, and almond extract. Allow this to stand while you prepare the rest of the dumplings.

In a large mixing bowl, sift together the flour, baking powder and salt. Cut in 4 tablespoons of the butter until fine crumbs are formed. In a small bowl, beat the egg and add the milk. Combine with the flour mixture and stir until just blended. Dot the cherries with the remaining 2 tablespoons of butter. Drop the batter by heaping tablespoons on top of the cherries—you should have 6 mounds. In a small bowl combine the remaining 2 tablespoons of sugar with the nutmeg. Sprinkle on top of the batter. Bake for 25 or 30 minutes, or until the fruit is bubbling up in the middle of the pan and the dumplings are golden brown.

The baking time can vary quite a bit, depending on the pan you use and how big the cherries are.

Makes six servings

Heartland: The Best of the Old and New from Midwest Kitchens

Tapawingo's Cherry Cobbler
with Rum Whipped Cream

Filling:

4 cups pitted tart cherries or 1 20-oz.
      bag frozen pitted cherries,
      thawed

$3/4$ cup sugar

2 tablespoons cornstarch

1 tablespoon fresh lemon juice

$1^1/2$ teaspoons grated lemon peel

$1/2$ teaspoon ground cinnamon

$1/4$ teaspoon ground nutmeg

3 tablespoons unsalted butter

Cobbler Topping:

1 cup all purpose-flour

$1/4$ cup sugar

1 $1/2$ teaspoons baking powder

$1/2$ teaspoon salt

2 tablespoons ($1/4$ stick) chilled
      unsalted butter, cut into pieces

$2/3$ cup whipping cream

1 tablespoon butter, melted

2 tablespoons sugar

Whipped Cream:

$1/2$ cup crème fraiche or sour cream

$1/4$ cup packed golden brown sugar

1 cup chilled whipping cream

2 tablespoons dark rum

For Filling: Preheat oven to 400 degrees. Butter 9-inch round baking dish. Combine first 7 ingredients in bowl. Pour into prepared dish. Dot with butter. Set aside.

For Cobbler Topping: Combine first 4 ingredients in medium bowl. Add 2 tablespoons chilled butter and cut in until coarse meal forms. Add whipping cream and stir until soft dough forms. Roll out dough on lightly floured surface to 6-inch square. Cut dough into twelve 2 x $1^1/2$-inch rectangles. Arrange dough rectangles side by side atop cherry filling in dish. Brush dough with 1 tablespoon melted butter and sprinkle with sugar. Bake until biscuits are puffed and golden brown, about 30 minutes. Cool cobbler slightly.

For Whipped Cream: Mix crème fraîche and sugar in large bowl until sugar dissolves. Add cream and rum and beat until soft peaks form. Serve cobbler warm with whipped cream.

Serves six

Tapawingo, Ellsworth, Michigan

Cherry Turtle Brownie

2 cups sugar, granulated

6 eggs, large

1 1/2 cups butter, softened

2 tablespoons cocoa powder

1/2 teaspoon salt

10 ounces semi-sweet chocolate
(chips)

1/2 cup corn syrup

1 cup sweet cherries, chopped
coarsely

1 1/2 cups pecans, chopped

2 cups all-purpose flour

Cherry ganache topping:

1 1/2 cups heavy cream

16 ounces semi- sweet chocolate,
chopped

1/2 cup butter

1/2 cup cherry juice concentrate

1/4 cup Kirsch (cherry liqueur)

1 jar caramel sauce

Preheat oven to 350 degrees.

For brownie: Using the paddle attachment to a mixer, lightly cream cocoa, sugar and butter. Add eggs two at a time until well blended. Do not over mix. Add melted chocolate and blend in well. Add corn syrup and the cherries and mix in. Add pecans and the flour. Mix until just blended. Scrape bowl and mix again. Pour batter into a 9 x 13 inch baking pan. Bake at 350 until a toothpick inserted into the center comes out clean, about 45 to 50 minutes. Cool and cover with cherry ganache, caramel sauce and chopped pecans.

For cherry ganache:
In medium pan, heat heavy cream over medium-low heat until a film forms on the top. Add the remaining ingredients and stir until well blended. Top brownies.

Serves sixteen

Northwestern Michigan College Culinary Arts Department

In 1952, about the vintage of this postcard, 70 floats, 22 marching bands and a record crowd of 225,000 people took part in the National Cherry Festival parade.

Susan Selasky's Apple Pie with Dried Cherries and Walnuts

Crust:

2 1/2 cups all-purpose flour

1/2 teaspoon salt

1 tablespoon brown sugar, optional

1/2 cup (1 stick) cold unsalted butter, cut into pieces

5 tablespoons cold shortening, cut into pieces

1 1/2 teaspoons cider vinegar

5 tablespoons ice water

Filling:

6 to 7 medium tart apple, peeled, cored and sliced (about 8 cups slices)

1/2 cup sugar

1/2 cup packed brown sugar

2 tablespoons all-purpose flour

1 teaspoon cornstarch

1 teaspoon cinnamon

1/4 teaspoon nutmeg

1 tablespoon unsalted butter

2 tablespoons apple juice or cider

1/3 cup dried cherries

1/3 cup toasted walnuts, chopped

Glaze:

1 tablespoon milk or half-and-half

1 teaspoon sugar

Preheat oven to 425 degrees.

For crust: In a mixing bowl, combine the flour, salt and brown sugar. Cut in the butter and shortening pieces until the mixture resembles coarse crumbs. Add the cider vinegar and the water 1 to 2 tablespoons at a time until the mixture holds together. Alternately, pulse the dry ingredients in a food processor, then pulse in the butter and shortening and add the liquid until a dough forms. Divide dough in half, shape into discs and wrap in plastic wrap. Place in the refrigerator while making the filling.

For filling: In a large mixing bowl, place the apple slices. In a separate small bowl, combine the sugar, brown sugar, flour, cornstarch, cinnamon and nutmeg. Cut in the butter pieces until the mixture forms coarse crumbs. Sprinkle the sugar mixture over the apples along with the apple juice. Toss gently to combine. Set aside.

Remove one dough disc to a lightly floured work surface. Roll out dough to a 12-inch circle to fit a 9-inch pie plate with the dough hanging over the edge. Place the filling in the pie shell. Roll out

Susan Selasky, *Detroit Free Press* test kitchen director

the remaining dough disc for the top crust. Fold in the edges and crimp. Cut slits in the top of the pie so steam vents. Mix together the half-and-half and sugar for the glaze. Brush on top of the pie.

Place the pie in the lower third of the oven for 15 minutes. Reduce heat to 375 degrees and continue baking until top crust is browned and filling is bubbly. If the edges brown too quickly, place aluminum foil over them.

Remove the pie from the oven and allow to cool at least 1 hour.

Cook's note: Hidden little gems of dried cherries show up in the filling of this pie, nestled between layers of apples. The addition of toasted and chopped walnuts is also a good match. For a basic pie crust, I like to use a blend of butter and shortening, which produces a rich, semi-flaky crust. Give the butter and shortening a good chill in the freezer for about 10 to minutes before adding to the flour.

Serves eight

Kathleen Sheridan's Old-Fashioned Cherry Tart

$1/2$ cup of all-purpose flour

1 sheet frozen puff pastry, $17^1/4$ ounce package, thawed

5 tablespoons unsalted butter, room temperature

$1/3$ cup plus 4 teaspoons of sugar

1 large egg

$1/2$ teaspoon almond extract

1 large egg yolk

2 tablespoons heavy cream

1 pounds fresh or frozen cherries, pitted

Preheat the oven to 425 degrees.

Line a surface with parchment paper, sprinkle lightly with flour. Roll out puff pastry to a $1/8$-inch thickness on the paper. Cut a 12-inch circle out of the dough. Roll up edges, making a 10-inch crust. Transfer parchment and crust to a baking sheet, and transfer to the refrigerator to chill, about 30 minutes. Place butter, $1/3$ cup sugar, flour, egg and almond extract in bowl; mix until combined. Remove crust from refrigerator; prick entire surface with a fork. In a small bowl, combine egg yolk and heavy cream to make an egg wash; brush the egg wash evenly over the surface and edges of the crust. Using a spatula, spread the almond mixture evenly in a $1/8$- inch thick layer in the bottom of the crust; chill 15 minutes more.

Remove the tart from the refrigerator and spread the cherries in a single layer over the almond mixture. Bake 15 minutes. Sprinkle the remaining 1 tablespoon plus 1 teaspoon of sugar over the tart and continue baking until the edges turn deep golden brown, 5 to 10 minutes. Transfer to a wire rack to cool. Serve warm or at room temperature.

Kathleen Sheridan is a Birmingham, Michigan food stylist and writer.

Oatmeal Cherry Cookies

1 cup (2 sticks) butter or margarine, softened
1 cup firmly packed brown sugar
1/2 cup granulated sugar
2 eggs
1 teaspoon pure vanilla extract
1 1/2 cups all-purpose flour
1 teaspoon baking powder
1/2 teaspoon salt (optional)
2 cups quick-cooking or old-fashioned oats, uncooked
1 1/2 cups dried tart cherries
1 cup semisweet chocolate chips

Preheat oven to 350 degrees.

Put margarine, brown sugar and granulated sugar in a large mixing bowl. Beat with an electric mixer on medium speed 3 to 4 minutes, or until creamy. Add eggs and vanilla; beat well. Combine flour, baking powder and salt, if desired; add to egg mixture. Stir in oats, cherries and chocolate chips; mix well.

Drop by rounded tablespoonfuls onto an ungreased cookie sheet. Bake for 10 to 12 minutes, or until golden brown. Let cool 1 minute on cookie sheet; remove to wire rack to cool completely. Store in a tightly covered container.

Makes about four dozen

Cherry Marketing Institute

Cherry Caramel Nut Bar

2 cups graham cracker crust
4 cups coconut flakes
$1/2$ cup cherry juice concentrate
1 cup dried cherries, chopped fine
1 cup sweetened condensed milk
3 cup walnuts, chopped
16 ounces caramel sauce

Preheat oven to 350 degrees.

Pack graham cracker crust on the bottom of a lightly greased 9 x 13 inch baking pan. In a medium bowl, mix coconut with the cherry concentrate and dried cherries. Cover the graham crackers with the coconut mixture.

Drizzle the coconut with the condensed milk. Pack the nuts on top of the coconut. Cover with the caramel sauce.

Bake until set, about 25 minutes.

Serves sixteen

Northwestern Michigan College Culinary Arts Department

Tapawingo's Tart Red Cherry Granita

4 cups tart cherries, pitted and finely
    chopped
1 cup dry white wine
3/4 cup granulated sugar
3 tablespoons Kirsch
Juice of 1/2 lemon

Equipment needed: Ice cream maker.

Finely chop the cherries by hand, or in food processor or blender, reserving all the juice. Make a simple syrup by mixing and bringing the wine and sugar just to the boil in a small saucepan. The sugar should have completely dissolved. Chill this syrup, then mix it into the cherries, their juice, the Kirsch and lemon juice. Freeze in an ice cream machine according to the manufacturer's instructions.

A coarse granita can also be made by pouring it into a flat dish and freezing in a regular freezer. The mixture must be stirred every half hour, until firm. In either case, the resulting ice is a tart, crystalline granita, appropriate as a mid-dinner refresher course.

Options: Honey can be substituted for the sugar, and there is no need to bring syrup to a boil. Fresh chopped mint (to taste) can be added before freezing.

*Makes about sixteen small sorbet
servings, or eight dessert servings*

Tapawingo, Ellsworth, Michigan

Napolean Motors Company churned out 95 passenger cars and 25 trucks in their manu-
facturing plant near Traverse City's Boardman River in 1918. By 1920, the company produced only trucks such as these 32-horsepower, $3/4$-ton trucks priced at $1,085. They found
their way to Morgan's Orchard, or so it seems in this Orson W. Peck postcard. It was
altered by Mr. Peck, who duplicated the image of one truck to give the effective appearance of the Napolean Truck cherry convoy seen here. The Napolean Motor Company closed
in 1923.

Cherry Sour Cream Pie

1 9-inch pie crust (your favorite pie crust recipe)

Pie Filling:
1 cup sour cream
$1/2$ cup sugar
2 tablespoons cornstarch
2 eggs, lightly beaten
$1/2$ teaspoon vanilla
$1/8$ teaspoon nutmeg
$1/2$ teaspoon cinnamon
5 cups cherries, fresh, pitted or frozen
$1^1/2$ cups streusel (recipe follows)

Streusel:
$1/2$ cup butter (1 stick)
$1/4$ cup brown sugar
$1/3$ cup sugar
$1/4$ teaspoon salt
$1/2$ teaspoon cinnamon
$1/2$ teaspoon vanilla
2 cups pastry flour (or all-purpose flour)

Preheat oven to 425 degrees.

For pie filling:
Mix sour cream, sugar and cornstarch until smooth. Add the eggs, vanilla and spices. Mix well. Carefully fold the cherries into the sour cream mixture. Fill unbaked pie shell. Top with the streusel. Bake for about 30 minutes or until filling is set.

For streusel:
Rub all the ingredients together using your fingers until the mixture is thoroughly blended and appears crumbly.

Makes one 9-inch pie

Northwestern Michigan College Culinary Arts Department

Brandied Cherries

2 pounds fresh sweet cherries,
    stemmed and pitted
2 cups sugar
1 quart brandy

Combine cherries, sugar and brandy; mix well. Store in tightly covered jar in a cool place for 6 or more weeks.

Serve over ice cream. Dress up cheesecake with a spoonful of cherries. Top flan with brandy and cherries. Spoon cherries over pound cake and top with whipped cream or cream fraiche. Combine with fruit in season and serve with special cookies. Dress up bread puddings with a topping of brandied cherries. Add to your favorite chocolate cake or brownie batter.

Makes about 1 $^1/_2$ quarts.

Washington State Fruit Commission

Black Cherry Compote

2 cups water
1 cup dried tart cherries
$1/2$ vanilla bean, split lengthwise
2 pounds frozen unsweetened pitted
    dark sweet cherries, thawed,
    juice reserved
$2/3$ cup honey
1 cinnamon stick
3 whole cloves
1 teaspoon grated lemon peel

Combine 2 cups water and dried cherries in large saucepan. Bring to boil. Reduce heat; simmer until water is reduced to $1/4$ cup, about 15 minutes.

Scrape in seeds from vanilla bean; add bean. Stir in dark cherries with juices and remaining ingredients. Simmer until cherries are tender and juices thicken, about 50 minutes. Cool.

(Can be made 3 days ahead. Cover and chill. Serve at room temperature.)

When in season, fresh cherries can be used in place of the frozen ones.

Use atop pound cake or angle food cake.

Makes about three and a half cups.

Bon Appétit May 1999

Peachy's Cherry Clafoutis

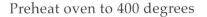

1½ pounds sweet dark cherries,
   washed, drained, dried and
   pitted
¾ cup flour
6 eggs
1 cup milk
dash of salt
1 tablespoon kirsch
½ cup sugar

Preheat oven to 400 degrees

Beat the eggs with the flour and salt. Add a little milk, beating constantly. Continue adding milk slowly while beating until you have a thin batter. Stir in cherries and kirsch. Pour the batter into a ceramic tart pan or pie plate and bake for 35 to 40 minutes. Serve warm or cold with granulated sugar or powdered sugar sprinkled over the top.

Serves eight

La Bécasse, Burdickville, Michigan near Glen Lake

Cherry Shortcake

Filling:
$1/3$ cup granulated sugar
1 tablespoon cornstarch
$1/8$ teaspoon cinnamon
1 pound fresh sweet cherries, washed
     and pitted
$1/4$ teaspoon lemon zest

Biscuits:
2 cups all-purpose flour
3 tablespoons sugar
2 $1/2$ teaspoons baking powder
$1/2$ teaspoon salt
$1/2$ cup (1 stick) butter, cut into pieces
$3/4$ cup buttermilk

Whipped cream topping:
1 cup heavy cream
3 tablespoons powdered sugar

For filling:
Mix granulated sugar, cornstarch and cinnamon in a saucepan. Add cherries and cook over medium heat, stirring until mixture thickens. Remove from heat; stir in lemon zest. Set aside.

Preheat oven to 400 degrees.

For biscuits:
Mix flour, sugar, baking powder and salt in a medium bowl. Add butter pieces and cut into flour mixture with pastry blender or fork until mixture is crumbly. Add buttermilk and mix just until moistened. Form dough into ball. On lightly floured surface, pat dough into a flattened disk about $3/4$-inch thick With a 2 $1/2$-inch round biscuit cutter, cut out 4 biscuits. Combine dough scraps and repeat to make 2 more biscuits. Arrange biscuits on ungreased baking sheet, and bake 18 to 20 minutes or until golden brown. Cool on a wire rack. Just before serving, whip heavy cream with powdered sugar until mixture holds soft peaks. To serve, cut biscuits horizontally in half. Place bottoms on serving plates, spoon cherry filling over shortcake and top with whipped cream. Cover with biscuit tops.

Serves six

173

Chocolate/Cherry Truffle Torte
with Michigan Tart Cherries

Torte:

4 ounces Michigan dried tart cherries
(scant 1 cup)

1/2 cup Kirsch, cherry brandy, or
cherry juice

12 ounces unsalted butter, cut into
tablespoons

12 ounces bittersweet chocolate,
chopped

3/4 cup granulated sugar

1/2 teaspoon almond extract

6 large eggs, at room temperature

Chocolate glaze:

2/3 cup whipping cream

8 ounces bittersweet chocolate, finely
chopped

2 tablespoons unsalted butter,
softened

Making the torte:

Preheat the oven to 325 degrees. Lightly butter the bottom and sides of a standard round 9 x 1 1/2-inch cake pan. Lightly butter, and line the bottom of the pan with a circle of baking parchment.

Roughly chop the cherries. In a heavy, medium saucepan over low heat, combine the butter, chocolates and sugar. Using a wooden spoon, stir frequently until sugar is dissolved and the mixture is smooth. Remove the pan from the heat. Stir in the Kirsch and almond extract. Whisk in the eggs, one at a time. Stir in the chopped dried cherries.

Pour the mixture into the prepared pan. Set the pan in a large roasting pan in the oven and pour hot water into the roasting pan to come halfway up the sides of the cake pan. Bake the torte for 50 to 60 minutes, or until a toothpick inserted into the center comes out clean.

Cool the torte in the pan on a wire rack 2 to 3 hours, until room temperature. Cover with plastic wrap and refrigerate 3 to 4 hours, until thoroughly chilled.

Serves twelve

Tapawingo, Ellsworth, Michigan

In a heavy, small saucepan over low heat, bring the cream to a boil. Remove the pan from the heat and whisk in the chocolate and butter. Stir until smooth. Strain the mixture through a fine sieve into a medium bowl, cover with plastic wrap, and let cool to room temperature, or to a nice glazing consistency.

Final Assembly: Run a knife around the sides of the torte to release it from the pan and invert it onto a cooling rack. Remove the parchment. Carefully pour the glaze over the top and sides of the torte, distributing evenly with a small spatula. Recover the excess glaze and chill to a pudding-like consistency. Fill a pastry bag with this glaze and pipe 12 rosettes around the top edge of the torte. Serve a small wedge, with barely sweetened whipped cream. Note: At times, I have unmolded the torte onto a thin, and very delicate almond shortbread layer, before glazing. This pastry layer does make for a nice detail, texture and appearance-wise. See the following shortbread recipe.

Almond Shortbread
5 ounces flour
2 tablespoons sugar
4 ounces butter in $1/2$-inch pieces
1 egg yolk
5 ounces ground blanched almonds

Preheat the oven to 375 degrees. Process flour, sugar and butter in food processor until blended. Add egg yolk and almonds. Pulse on and off for about 1 minute. Turn out on pastry table and form into a firm and smooth round. Between sheets of parchment, roll pastry to an even, 10-inch round, 3/8 inch thick. Remove top sheet of parchment, prick with fork, and place on baking sheet. Bake for about 15 minutes, or until the pastry is just set, and edges barely start to brown. Remove from oven and cool. The pastry is very delicate and must be handled carefully. When cool, trim the pastry to exactly fit the truffle torte.

Can she bake a cherry pie, Billy Boy, Billy Boy?
Can she bake a cherry pie, charming Billy?
She can bake a cherry pie, there's a twinkle in her eye,
She's a young thing and cannot leave her mother.

—American Folksong

Smooth Sippers

Black Cherry Punch

$1/2$ cup fresh lemon juice, strained
$1/2$ cup fresh orange juice, strained
$1/4$ cup fresh lime juice, strained
$1/4$ cup superfine granulated sugar
1 pound fresh black cherries, pitted
    (or a 17-ounce can pitted black
    cherries, drained)
2 cups light rum
$1/2$ cup dark rum
$1/2$ cup Cherry Herring
$1/2$ cup crème de cassis
4 cups chilled seltzer or club soda
Garnish: thin lime slices

In a large bowl, combine lemon juice, orange juice and lime juice. Stir in sugar and continue stirring until dissolved. Stir in cherries, light rum, dark rum, Cherry Herring and crème de cassis. Chill for 1 hour. Transfer to a punch bowl and stir in the seltzer. Add a block of ice or ice cubes. Garnish the punch with lime slices.

Makes eight cups

Gourmet August 1983

Restaurant Villegas'
Michigan Dried Tart Cherry Cosmopolitan

1 ounce **cherry** vodka, a few soaked
    cherries reserved for garnish
    (recipe below*)
$1/2$ ounce triple sec
$1/2$ ounce simple syrup
1 ounce Michigan tart cherry juice
    concentrate

*cherry vodka:
1 cup dried Michigan tart cherries
1 cup premium vodka

Cover the tart cherries in a
nonreactive container for 4-6 hours or
overnight. Strain, use as needed.

Combine all ingredients in a cocktail shaker with ice. Shake well and strain into a martini glass. Garnish with the vodka-soaked cherries.

Eric Villegas, chef-proprietor, Restaurant Villegas, Okemos, Michigan

Restaurant Villegas' Michigan Cherry and White Chocolate Cordial

1 oz. cherry vodka* (see recipe)
1¹/2 oz. Godiva white chocolate
    liqueur

*cherry vodka:
1 cup dried Michigan tart cherries
1 cup premium vodka

Cover the tart cherries in a nonreactive container for 4-6 hours or overnight. Strain, use as needed.

Combine the cherry vodka and white chocolate liqueur in a cocktail shaker with ice. Shake well and strain into a cordial glass.

From Eric Villegas, chef-proprietor, Restaurant Villegas, Okemos, Michigan

Simply Cherry Smoothie

2 cups frozen tart cherries
1 ripe banana
1 cup cherry juice blend

Combine frozen cherries, banana and cherry juice in a blender or food processer. Puree until smooth. Pour into individual serving glasses. Garnish with fresh strawberry of cherry.

Serves four

Cherry Marketing Institute

Banana-Orange Smoothie

2 8-ounce containers low-fat cherry
  yogurt
2 bananas, peeled, cut into pieces
2 oranges, peeled, white pith removed, cut into segments
16 frozen dark cherries
12 frozen strawberries

Combine 1 container yogurt, 1 banana, 1 orange, 8 cherries and 6 strawberries in blender. Blend on medium speed until smooth. Divide between 2 glasses. Repeat with remaining ingredients.

Makes four servings

Bon Appétit April 1994

Frozen Cranberry, Cherry and Orange Cocktail

1 cup cracked ice
1 pony (1 ounce) cranberry liqueur
1 pony (1 ounce) Cherry Herring
1 pony (1 ounce) Grand Marnier
1 tablespoon superfine granulated
     sugar, or to taste
Garnish: twist of orange

In a blender, blend cracked ice, cranberry liqueur, Cherry Herring, Grand Marnier and, if desired, sugar for 30 seconds. Pour into a chilled 12-ounce glass. Garnish with the twist of orange.

Serves one

Kathleen Sheridan's Berry-Vodka Cooler

1 10-ounce package frozen
    sweetened raspberries in
    syrup, thawed
1 10-ounce package frozen
    sweetened strawberries in
    syrup, thawed
$1/4$ cup fresh lemon juice
3 cups black cherry juice
2 cups currant-flavored vodka or
    plain vodka
2 cups sparkling water
3 cups ice cubes

Omit the alcohol for a kid-friendly
    drink.

Combine thawed raspberries with syrup, strawberries with syrup and lemon juice in blender. Puree until smooth. Strain liquid into pitcher; discard solids in strainer. Add cherry juice and vodka. Can be made 6 hours ahead.

Optional garnish: Fresh mint sprigs.

Kathleen Sheridan is a Birmingham, Michigan food stylist and writer.

184

Kathleen Sheridan's Cherry Capitol Smoothie

1 cup frozen pitted cherries
$1/2$ cup calcium fortified orange juice
2 tablespoons protein powder
1 carton (8 oz.) black-cherry yogurt
1 banana

Blend for one minute in a blender and serve.

Serves six to eight

Kathleen Sheridan is a Birmingham, Michigan food stylist and writer.

Kathleen Sheridan's Cherry Lemonade

$1^1/4$ cup fresh lemon juice (10 - 12 fresh lemons)

$1^1/2$ cup sugar

1 pound pitted fresh or frozen cherries

In a gallon pitcher, combine lemon juice and sugar until dissolved. Stir in three quarts of cold water and the cherries. Pour the lemonade into glasses with ice and serve.

Kathleen Sheridan is a Birmingham, Michigan food stylist and writer.

Sources For Cherry Products

American Spoon Foods, 411 East Lake St., Petoskey, MI 231-347-1739; 315 Bridge St., Charlevoix, MI 231-547-5222; 230 East Front St., Traverse City, MI 231-935-4480; Grand Traverse Resort, Traverse City, MI 231-938-5358; 245 East Main St., Harbor Springs, MI 231-526-8628; 308 Butler St., Saugatuck, MI 616-857-3084. General info: 800-222-5886. Dried, chocolate-covered, preserves, butters, marmalades, special gift boxes. www.spoon.com

Amon Orchards, 8066 US 31 N, PO Box 27, Acme, MI 49610-0027, 800-937-1644 or 231-938-9160. Cherry concentrate, dried fruit, jams and jellies, no-sugar jams, sauces, gift-box specials. www.amonorchards.com

Benjamin Twiggs, 1215 E. Front St., Traverse City, MI 49686, 877-236-8944. Dried fruit, chocolates, butters, dressings, marinades, sauces, salsas, toppings, pancakes, coffee, tea, cherry concentrate, gift baskets. www.benjamintwiggs.com

Brownwood Acres, at the north end of Torch Lake on US-31, Eastport, MI, 877-591-3101 or 231-599-3101. Juice concentrate, butters and spreads, preserves and marmalade, salsas, dried Cherries and honey, mustards and barbecue sauce. www.brownwoodacres.com

Cherry Marketing Institute, Inc., P.O. Box 30285, Lansing, MI 48909-7785. Sources across the country for cherry products. www.cherrymarketing.org

Cherry Point Farm Market, 9600 West Buchanan Rd., Shelby Mi. 49455, 231-861-2029 Fresh and dried fruit, strudel, jams and jelly, fudge. www.cherrypointmarket.com

Cherry Republic, Box 677, 6026 S. Lake St., Glen Arbor, MI 49636, 800-206-6949. Dried cherries, chocolate-covered cherries, cherry concentrate, nuts, mixes, baked goods and gift items. www.cherryrepublic.com

Cherry Station, 1707 Allied Lane, Charlottesville, VA 22902, 800-238-0349 or 434-817-1810. Dried and chocolate-covered, preserves, sauces, gift boxes, concentrate.

The Cherry Stop, 211 E. Front Traverse City, MI 49684, 231-929-3990. Mail order 800-286-7209. Retail and mail order for a large varity of cherry food products and gifts. Source for quality dried sweet and tart cherries, individual quick frozen tart and sweet cherries, and cherry juice concentrate. www.cherrystop.com

Chukar Cherry Co., 320 Wine Country Road, PO Box 510, Prosser, WA 99350-0510, 800-624-9544 or 509-786-2055. Grower and producer of dried fruits and nuts in natural and chocolate covered treats, pure fruit jams, toppings, pie fillings, and savories. Kosher. No sulfites, preservatives, artificial flavors or hydrogenated fats added.

Engle Ridge Farm, 6754 Yuba Rd., Williamsburg, MI 49690, 888-448-5817. Michigan Balaton Cherry products, a sweeter, larger, darker-hued tart cherry recently introduced to U.S. palates. Pie filling, butters, preserves, individually quick-frozen.

Frank Farms, 8249 Deans Hill Road, Berrien Center, MI 49102, 616-461-4125. U-pick farm. Cherry concentrate, dried and chocolate-covered dried cherries. www.frankfarms.com.

Leland Cherry Co., 106 Lake Street - Suite 2, Leland, Michigan 49654, 800-939-3199 or 231-256-2033. Cherry concentrate, gift baskets, dried fruit, jams, jellies, no-sugar jams, sauces. www.lelandcherry.com

Pleva's Meats: Ray Pleva has been on Oprah and Home Improvement, tirelessly promoting all things cherry. That's why he is known as Mr. Cherry, for his cherry sausages and low-fat Plevalean burgers. Buy it and other innovative cherry things at this Leelanau County Market at 8974 S. Kasson St., Cedar, Michigan 231-228-5000

Stone House Bread, 407 South Main St., Leland, 231-256-2577 or 800-252-3218; also available throughout Northern Michigan and the Detroit-Ann Arbor area. Owner Bob Pisor's cherry-walnut bread makes great French toast. www.stonehousebread.com

Underwood Fruit, P.O. Box 6633, Traverse City, MI 49686-9903, 888-947-4047, 231-922-2866. Cherry Rich wafers and capsules for arthritis, chocolate-covered and dried fruit, cherry concentrate.

Index

C

Notes:

Bibliography

TAVERNA, The Best of Casual Mediterranean Cooking, Joyce Goldstein, Sunset Publishing Corporation, Menlo, CA., 1996.

Bon Appetit, published by CondeNast Publications Inc. Conde Nast Building, 4 Times Square, New York, N.Y., 10036.

Bountiful Arbor, Junior League of Ann Arbor, Ann Arbor, MI, 1994.

The Common Grill Cookbook, Craig Common, Sleeping Bear Press, Chelsea, MI, 2000.

Cooking for all Seasons, Jimmy Schmidt, Macmillan Publishing, New York, N.Y., 1991.

A Culinary Collection, The Detroit Institute of Arts Founders Society, Detroit, MI, 2000.

Gourmet Magazine, published by Conde Nast Publications Inc. Conde Nast Building, 4 Times Square, New York, N.Y., 10036.

Heartland: The Best of the Old and the New Midwest Kitchens, Marcia Adams, Clarkson N. Potter, New York, NY., 1991.

The Junior League Centennial Cookbook, The Association of Junior Leagues International Inc., Doubleday, New York, N.Y., 1996.

Keith Famie's Adventures in Cooking, Keith Famie, Sleeping Bear Press, Chelsea, MI, 2001.

Leelanau Country Inn Cookery...Continued: Food and wine from the land of delight. Linda and John Sisson. Bucca Press, Maple City, MI., 2000.

Praire Home Cooking, Judith M. Fertig, 1999, The Harvard Common Press, Boston, MA , 1999.

Recipes from Morroco, Mary MacKillop, Michele Wortman, 1994, Oliver Books, Hollywood, CA, 1994.

Patty LaNoue Stearns writes about food, travel and other lifestyle subjects for a number of publications across the country, including a weekly restaurant column in the *Traverse City Record-Eagle*. A former food columnist and restaurant critic for the *Detroit Free Press* and managing editor of *Detroit Monthly* magazine, Stearns has been a journalist for more than three decades, covering everything from cars to clothes to haute cuisine. She has contributed to the *Mobil Travel Guide* and *AAA Travel Guide* and is featured prominently in *Dining Out – Secrets from America's Leading Critics, Chefs and Restaurateurs* by Andrew Dornenburg and Karen Page (John Wiley & Sons). Stearns studied English and Journalism at the University of Detroit and culinary arts at Le Cordon Bleu, Paris, France.